I'm Shady so they

baby I like that

as CRAZY as

made me

Slim Shady

children

P R O O F

1 9 7 3 — 2 0 0 6

One thing we all adore

Something worth dying for

Nothing but pain

Stuck in this game

Searching for fortune and fame

— T U P A C   S H A K U R

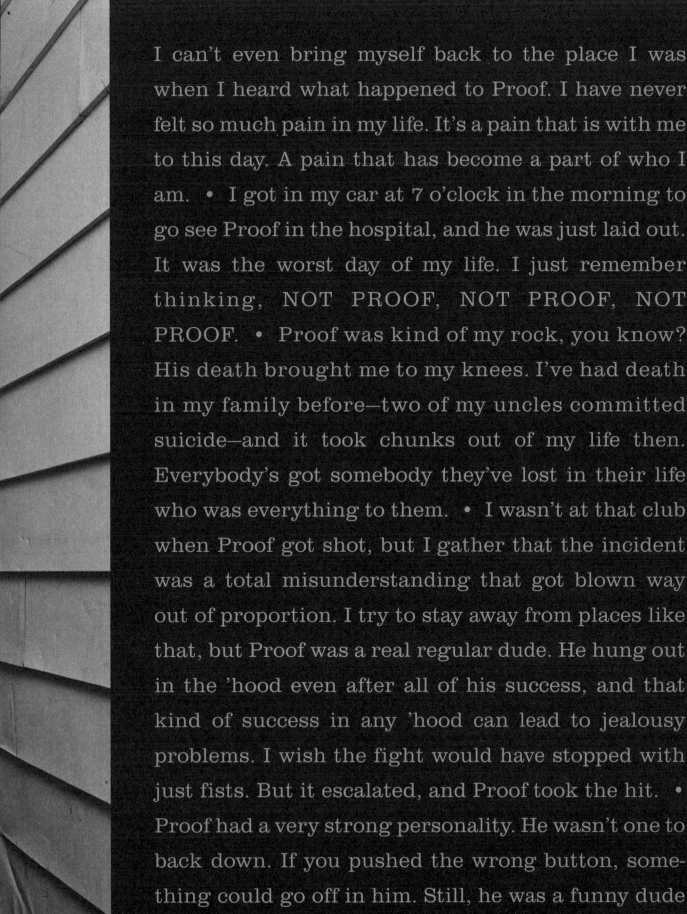

I can't even bring myself back to the place I was when I heard what happened to Proof. I have never felt so much pain in my life. It's a pain that is with me to this day. A pain that has become a part of who I am. • I got in my car at 7 o'clock in the morning to go see Proof in the hospital, and he was just laid out. It was the worst day of my life. I just remember thinking, NOT PROOF, NOT PROOF, NOT PROOF. • Proof was kind of my rock, you know? His death brought me to my knees. I've had death in my family before—two of my uncles committed suicide—and it took chunks out of my life then. Everybody's got somebody they've lost in their life who was everything to them. • I wasn't at that club when Proof got shot, but I gather that the incident was a total misunderstanding that got blown way out of proportion. I try to stay away from places like that, but Proof was a real regular dude. He hung out in the 'hood even after all of his success, and that kind of success in any 'hood can lead to jealousy problems. I wish the fight would have stopped with just fists. But it escalated, and Proof took the hit. • Proof had a very strong personality. He wasn't one to back down. If you pushed the wrong button, something could go off in him. Still, he was a funny dude who wasn't gangsta *all* the time. He had a silly side, like all of us in D12 do. • So although Proof had this dual personality, what I remember most is his kindness. This is the dude who, when I was broke as fuck, came by my house and made me get rid of the thrift-store loafers my mother had bought me. We're both size 10. He came over to the crib and was like, "What the fuck is on your feet?" Then he handed over a pair of Nikes that were pretty much brand new. It was one of those moments where I wanted to cry. • Just like all friends do, Proof and I went through our up and down phases. On the road we'd be with each other 24/7, and when we'd get back to The D, we would take time off. Because, you know, I can be an annoying motherfucker just like everybody else. If I didn't see him for a while we would at least talk on the phone a couple times a week. We'd both become family men, too, and we'd be busy with our kids. • After he passed, it was a year before I could really do anything normally again. It was tough for me to even get out of bed, and I had days when I couldn't walk, let alone write a rhyme. When I tried to put my thoughts together—well, I wasn't making sense when I spoke, so everyone was trying to keep me off TV and away from the press. My brain was scattered, especially for the first couple of months after his death. • It's been only two years and change now since he left, so it's still a tough thing to deal with. Now, when I think about touring, I wonder who's going to come onstage with me. This is the biggest tragedy I could imagine, aside from something happening to one of my kids. •

Proof played the fall guy in the video for "Like Toy Soldiers." The guy shot and in the hospital. The point I was trying to make with that video was that rappers get into beefs, but it's really the opposing camps—the entourages—who wind up getting hurt. Not too long after that, it unfortunately became reality. • In the year after he died, I would stare at the ceiling and think about that video. Did karma cause that to happen in real life? Did I? You always want to point the finger at somebody else when something like that happens, you know? • Proof was the key to my whole game. He was the only reason I stopped getting my ass whipped. I'm not going to sugarcoat it—he was my ghetto pass. I don't know if anybody realizes it; that's why I'm saying it now. He didn't give a fuck about being called an Uncle Tom for being down with me. He stuck up for me like we were literally brothers. Before I was famous, before I had anything, really, Kim and I were living in her mom's attic because we had nowhere else to go. If Proof hadn't gotten me out of there, if he hadn't gotten me down to The Hip Hop Shop and into the rap game, I don't know where I'd be. I certainly wouldn't be somebody you've heard of. • He was a brilliant cat who saw things in me that I didn't see yet, and I guess I was smart enough to understand that he was the dude who could somehow save my life. I had been drowning for so long. Proof was like a hip-hop life raft and a true brother from another mother. He had this ability to not only nurture my talent, but to see that diamond in the rough when a million people could be looking at the same thing and just not see it. • It's not like Proof didn't have plenty of his own talent to deal with. Proof was a hip-hop dude nobody could fuck with. Freestyling, battling—nobody could fuck with him. Nobody. • He used to come with us on the radio—Friday nights were open mic in Detroit. This is when I was with my first group, called Bassmint Productions. We had a song with Proof we were performing on air, and Proof hadn't learned his verse by heart yet. He only remembered his first four lines, and then he just started freestyling. You couldn't even tell that he fucked up because he was so good at it. That was Proof's God-given gift, to be able to freestyle like that. • Proof controlled the entire Motor City rap music scene in the mid- to late-'90s. He was that dude with dreads from Detroit who knew everybody. And everybody swore that he was going to be the first solo rapper to really make it out of Detroit. • I remember seeing Treach and Vinnie from Naughty by Nature at his funeral. I thanked them for coming out, but in hindsight I realized, Wow, why did I thank them? They were there for him—not me. Everyone was. • I was looking at it like, this was my best friend, so some people were there to support me in my loss. But he obviously had his own deep connections and relationships. People liked him—loved him. So I lost my best friend, but I guarantee you there's a million people who would say, "Yeah, well, Proof was my best friend too." • But with Proof and me, it was a mutual feeling. That's why I say, "That was my best friend; I was his best friend."

Ǝ
THE WAY I AM

EMI

1

ALL I KNOW, PART 1

I KNEW I WANTED TO BE A RAPPER WHEN I WAS AROUND 14.

That's the same year I met Proof. It was just like I said in "Yellow Brick Road." I was on the steps of Osborn High, where Proof went to school, handing out flyers for a talent show: "I had told him to stop by / And check this out sometime / He looked at me like I'm out of my mind shook his head like white boys don't know how to rhyme / I spit out a line and rhymed birthday with first place / And we both had the same rhymes that sound alike / We was on the same shit that Big Daddy Kane shit with compound syllables sound combined / From that day we was down to ride somehow we knew we'd meet again somewhere down the line."

At Osborn, Proof used to sneak me into the lunchroom to battle and hustle the fools there. We got paid. Proof would say, "I got 20 bucks on the white boy." It was the *White Men Can't Jump* theory—no one thought the white boy could win. Proof would start banging a beat on the table, and we'd go around and I'd beat everybody who wanted to battle. Straight up. We'd go home and split up the money. We used to clean up—it was almost like we were pool sharks. But people started getting hip to that game, so we had to come up with a new one.

That's when I started painting on jeans and jackets. Proof would kill me if he knew I was telling people this, but his first rap name was Maximum. So I painted "Maximum" on his jeans. I was serious with the art. I'd squeeze the fabric paint out to make the borders of the letters, then paint inside. I stole the paint—I used to be a little klepto. I would wear a fluffy down jacket, full of feathers and shit, and it had mad pockets. So I would fill up my coat with little bottles of fabric paint.

My clientele were cats Proof would bring from the neighborhood. He would tell me what people wanted and I'd say, "What do you think I should charge?" If it was $60, I would give Proof a 20 spot. Back then that was a lot of money for me, it was like a second job. Better than the factory I was working at, sandblasting and doing dishes in the kitchen and cleaning machinery, getting my hands eaten up.

Early on Proof brought me one guy who wanted "Eazy-E" on the back of his stonewashed jean jacket. "Eazy-E" with a gun. When I started out on that painting I didn't realize how long it was going to take. More and more people wanted stuff painted, and the orders started backing up. Proof was saying, "Yo, the homie wants his

Eazy-E jacket. When are you gonna be finished?" "Eazy" took up the entire back of the jean jacket. The whole thing probably took 20 bottles of the paint that I stole.

Proof taught me to stand up and be a man. He was the first person to show me how to fight. If you've never been hit, you're scared to be hit because you don't know what it's going to feel like. Proof got me over that initial fear. He and I would bare-knuckle box. My shots would be so wide open that Proof would just keep tagging me. At Dresden Street, there was a redneck biker dude who used to stand at the fence and watch us fight. He'd be like, "Come on, Marshall, get up! What are you, a pussy? Get up!" And Proof would go, "Damn, stay down, man, stay down." But I'd always get right the fuck back up. Until Proof would knock me completely senseless. I just told him, "Don't knock my teeth out! Please?!"

He was constantly keeping me on my Ps and Qs. We'd come inside the house afterward with bloody knuckles, tired and fucked up. From there, Proof would make us do this drill where one of us would pick a word and then see how many words we could rhyme with it. Or pick five words and make a rhyme in one minute. And whoever didn't get it done would get punched in the face. (Kidding.)

We fought like brothers, but we could never have a real beef. There was a bond that just could not be broken. We would fight about the stupidest things. Once, I didn't pick up Proof when I said I would because I was talking to this girl on the phone for a hot minute. When I finally showed up, Proof said he didn't want to play hoops anymore. I tossed him the ball and motioned for him to get in the front seat.

He threw it on the floor of my car, shut the door, and stormed off. We didn't speak for two weeks. It was weird because we both worked at the same place then—Little Caesars. One day he comes by and snaps me right in the ass with a towel. I'm like, "You motherfucker!" I run at him and we start having this towel war. All of a sudden, we're friends again.

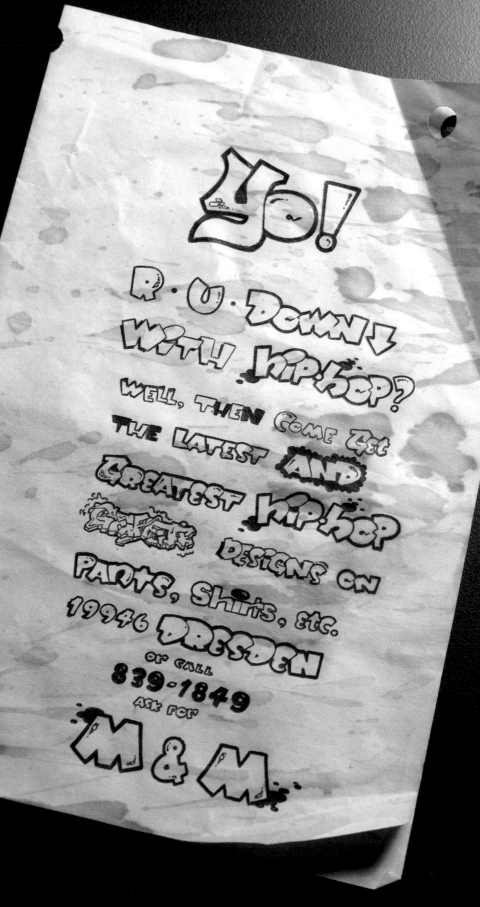

My uncle Ronnie first turned me on to hip-hop when I was 11. My grandmother had him late in life, so even though he was my uncle we were about the same age, and we grew up together as kids in Missouri. Ronnie made tapes by himself. He lived in this trailer park, and he had two radios with cassette decks. He used one as a beat box. He hit play—I remember exactly how it went—then he hit record on the other deck, and rapped over the beat. "That faggot walking down the street / He think that he have a funky beat / Huh-huh, look at him, combing his hair / I bet he don't even change his underwear / He thinks he's bad, I think he's sad / But the only reason I am glad / I am the king of the funky beat / I know what's going down." I made a copy and took that tape home and listened to it over and over. That's when I realized I wanted to do it myself: rap. I hadn't touched hip-hop yet. I was into Michael Jackson and New Edition, you know, "Cool It Now." But even in "Cool It Now" they rapped at the end. I had heard raps before then—the first one was "Jam on It" by Newcleus—on the radio. And Ronnie had brought over the *Breakin'* soundtrack with Ice-T's "Reckless" on it. After I heard his tapes, I started grabbing everything, older rap like Mantronix. I memorized the lyrics to "The Message." It was all starting to sink in.

At the beginning of 6th grade, three kids I went to school with taught me to break dance. They would throw down a piece of cardboard in the school library and get busy. We were living in these public housing apartments in Savannah, Missouri, and my friends and I used to walk with our cardboard to the playground up the street, set the cardboard down—and we'd attract all the girls who lived in the complex. That was the shit!

I didn't see Uncle Ronnie for a while, because my mom moved us back to Detroit. When we visited Missouri for a summer, Ronnie had gotten into heavy metal and cowboy boots. It just bugged me the fuck out. I knew the words to LL Cool J's "I'm Bad" front and back. And I'm standing in Ronnie's driveway, rapping it, putting on a show for cars riding by. No one could tell me I wasn't LL Cool J!

The Beastie Boys' *License to Ill* played a big part for me. Because obviously, they were white guys rapping in a predominantly black music form. And they were just fun. One of the best live hip-hop shows I ever saw as a kid was Run-DMC's Tougher than Leather tour. The Beastie Boys opened the show, and they brought a giant dick out onstage. Hip-hop was so live back then. Performance meant everything. If you were wack you'd get booed off the stage. Because hip-hop always keeps it real.

I liked the Beastie Boys because they were themselves—they weren't fronting. Millions of kids around the world could relate to where they were coming from. When they first came out, they had mad respect in the underground. They had it all covered. It was them being themselves that helped me figure out how to relax and be me. Made me feel like I could get up there and rock the mic and rock millions. That's what every wannabe rapper wants.

I spent a lot of time by myself, so hip-hop became my girl, my confidant, my best homie. It had so many emotions: LL could rap about the girls, and Rakim, with his wordplay, could get real deep with it. Boogie Down Productions could actually teach you something—which is incredible when you're just listening to music for the vibe. Masta Ace had amazing storytelling skills—his thoughts were so vivid.

HIP-HOP BECAME MY GIRL, MY CONFIDANT, MY BEST HOMIE.

Emcees were real people who dressed like you did. They wore Adidas just like you. And hip-hop was raw, it was so direct. I understood the language. It was putting words together and talking shit—the shit that was on my mind, be it funny or angry or sad. It gave me confidence when people were into what I was saying. Helped me communicate better with girls. It was rhythmic, and rhythmic things—like basketball—help me to express myself.

All of these rappers and groups were my teachers, and I was a full-time student of hip-hop. I think you can hear a bit of all of them in what I've done.

The first time I rapped at an actual club was when I was in my teens. I was pretty fucking young. It's one of those things where you want to try it out, see if you're okay with it. It was just terrible.

It was at a party called The Rhythm Kitchen. I went with some friends. Stupidly, not Proof. I was trying to poke fun at myself, and I said something in a rap like "cracker" or "honky." For some reason I thought that it would be cool for the crowd to chant, and it was a pretty big mistake. I might have gotten three words out and immediately the jeering started. That was one of my worst experiences. I thought, Oh fuck! I'm not good at this. I went home with my tail between my legs.

It took me a long time after that to perform in public again, but I kept rapping. I was making songs whenever I could, but because our equipment was so ghetto, I'd have to nail it in one take. If I messed up, I'd have to do it all over again from the top. So I had to not only write the song, but learn it by heart. Back then, I was with a group called Bassmint Productions—my first rap group. We would take the finished product up to Lisa Lisa and this guy named DJ Dick—they were radio personalities in Detroit and had a show called "Open Mic" every Friday night. They gave us our first shot, telling people to check us out.

Mark Bass heard our song called "Crackers and Cheese" on the radio and he liked it. He and his brother Jeff had a studio, F.B.T., the Funky Bass Team. He called up Lisa Lisa and asked, "Who is that?" We talked to him on the air, and then we ended up going to his studio, and we made a three-song demo.

I was too young. It was too early in my career. The Bass Brothers had a connection, and they played it for some folks at Elektra Records. The label said, "Eminem sounds too young." My voice was real squeaky. (Not that it wasn't on "My Name Is," but I'll get to that soon.)

I took my income tax refunds and a little bit of extra money and started paying to record more at F.B.T. Mark Bass came in and listened to the stuff, and he liked it. So he

I was driving my Mercury Tracer, going around to record stores, putting my tapes on consignment. That's how it started.

started letting me in little by little, sometimes to record for free. He saw I was taking initiative. I made my own cassette tapes and released my own singles. I drew the cover, my own artwork. It was a cartoon cover, and the songs were called "Fuckin' Backstabber" and "Biterphobia."

When I got the tapes, I didn't even know what to do with them. I started going around, putting them on consignment at record stores, and they weren't selling. I think I sold maybe three copies of the shit. When I go back and listen to them now, they're wack, but I guess they weren't wack for that time period.

When I was 18, I was confused about which way to go with life: I was good at rap, but I wasn't great. I thought I could be better at basketball than I could be at rapping. I was seriously considering pursuing a pro b-ball career. I played pretty hard-core for that entire year. There were two courts I used to play at—one where I was the best baller and one where I was the second best, if this one dude showed up. He was taller than me, and he could dunk.

B-ball was a long shot, but so was rapping. Vanilla Ice had made it damn near impossible for a white kid to get respect in rap music. Proof and I wanted the dream, so we gambled big. We dropped out and went for the gold.

Proof quit his job at Little Caesars. He said, "Fuck this, I'm doing hip-hop full-time." He started growing his dreads out, and he was on his way to becoming the best-known hip-hop figure in all of Detroit.

Proof would come back to Little Caesars with his own group at the time, Five Elements. Once, we played each other our songs in the parking lot, and it was a defining moment for me, because it made me feel like I could keep up. Proof thought my song was better than his! He was like, "I gotta get back in the studio!" So there was competition between us, but it was positive. It helped me grow as a writer and artist. After that he'd come back

and play more songs. He was hanging around with Jaydee (J Dilla, R.I.P.) and getting beats from him. The sound was so clean, it made my shit sound bad by comparison. His beats were so dope. If you listen to those tapes, the way Proof rhymed still sounds dope. He had Tommy Boy Records looking at him, and was going back and forth to New York. Everyone just assumed Proof was going to be the first to get a solo record deal.

Around 1992, I moved to another place on the East Side of Detroit, on Novara Street. (I shout that street out in a couple of raps, like "Mockingbird.") We had a house full of bachelors. Even though I had a girl, she didn't stay there all the time. So I'd get off work at 11 o'clock, and we'd sit on the porch and drink 40s and rap against each other, or we'd freestyle. One of our roommates, my boy Butter, had a mic and a turntable.

Denaun Porter, who is Kon Artis in D12, used to stay there too. He ended up working at Little Caesars with us, and I gave him my bedroom so he could set up his equipment in there. I slept on the couch, which wasn't a big deal. It was a fair trade—the guy was making my beats. Then we'd go to real studios, like Mo Master, whenever we could get in. And you better nail your verse in one or two takes, because you've only got 40

bucks in your pocket, and it's 40 bucks an hour to book the studio.

Denaun also lived with me, Kim and Hailie on Fairport Street when Hailie was a newborn. Proof set up a little four-track studio in the basement. This is when the early essence of D12 was really starting to come together. We didn't even really know it yet. We were all friends and associates, mainly through Proof and the Detroit scene. There was Bizarre, of course—everyone knows Bizzy. Denaun and his friend Kuniva rhymed together and called themselves Da Brigade. Bugz introduced me to Swift, who was in a group called the Rabeez with Bareda—they were dope. We rapped and recorded together because sometimes it made sense economically. We had to share resources—shit has always been lean in the D.

With Denaun on the beats, the six of us would go hard on the rhymes. It was very competitive, as far as who got on what track, how much space there was for each rhymer. If I rapped a take and folks liked it, we would stop the tape and figure out who was gonna blaze it next. So everyone would just be standing around my basement waiting to get their chance. Everybody was so tight back then. We made this pact—the infamous pact. Whoever makes it out first will come back for the rest of us.

Rap was always a pipe dream for me, but rap was all I had. Because really, what was I going to do with my life? I had a young daughter. Kim and I were always either getting evicted or our house was getting shot up or robbed.

We had to move to Kim's parents' house for a while, up in the attic. You couldn't even stand up in it. We put a mattress on the floor and called it a bedroom. I'd listen to beats on the stereo up there and write rhymes. I started to become a little hermit-ish. I was thinking, All I have to do is make a new demo. I'll find out how to shop it. But I slowed down for a period. Just dealing with life shit, domestic shit. Proof was always on me, though. That's when he got me out of that attic. He called me one night and had me say one of those raps over the phone. He told me to come down to The Hip Hop Shop to see what kind of response I'd get. That's when everything changed.

I had recorded some stuff with this kid Skam—I talk about it in "Stan." He's a rapper but he's also a dope comic book artist, and he ended up doing all the album art for *The Slim Shady LP* and portraits of D12 the way we really look when we're just hanging out. That's Bizzy with the hip-hop beer mug. I'm the mummy representing the 313. Kuniva's rocking the spiked helmet, Kon Artis is carrying the crowbar, and Swifty's got the bag of cash. The crazy-looking robot is Proof. And DJ Head (in the jar) toured with us and was the house DJ at The Hip Hop Shop.

THE HIP WAS HUGE.

When Maurice Malone first opened The Hip Hop Shop it was mainly a clothing store. He started having open mic sessions there on Saturdays. Proof hosted it, doing battles and rhyming contests. Maurice was really supportive of the local scene. The Hip Hop Shop was like the Apollo—you could get booed out of there quicker than shit if you weren't paying attention. It was the place if you wanted to make a name for yourself, not only in Detroit but all over the world. And the crowd would not put up with bullshit. They heard bullshit, they flew.

Proof was a mastermind. He had it all planned that day. He told me that there was a big battle going down, and that I should get there at the end, when the shop was clearing out, so I could ease my way into it and get feedback from a smaller number of people. He said, "Come out and see if you like it. If you don't like it, you never have to come here again."

That's how I did it—I went there 20 minutes before the battle was over. This was in '95. I rapped and I got a response and it was *insane*. The people were jumping up and down and screaming. The heads there were like, "Proof, where did you find this dude at?"

I started going every single week, putting my work schedule around performing there. I built up the confidence to keep doing it, and then I started battling people. I was the only white dude rappin' in there and

I was getting *love*, finally getting the respect I had dreamed of. Even though it was in that small circle—it didn't matter. I finally had acceptance.

Feeding off that energy made me come back the next week, and the next week, and the next week. I became addicted to the oohs and ahhs from the audience. There'd be bigger and bigger crowds every time. I started getting a name for myself in Detroit and I actually got paid for shows. That was big for me.

I started really making moves after I connected with my manager, Paul Rosenberg, in '95. Proof introduced us—of course—when I won the second big annual battle at The Hip Hop Shop. (That was against La Peace, who I left in La Pieces.) Paul moved to New York to be a lawyer, but I

I kept the pass on my T-shirt to show that I had rocked with the Wu. Me and The Outsidaz opened for Wu-Tang at the Park Hill Housing Projects in Staten Island. I had met The Outsidaz through Bizarre, and when me and Paul took the bus to meet them in New Jersey, they warned us not to get off at the Newark station until we saw them—or we would get robbed. And I thought Detroit was heavy! I started getting booed when I first came out at Park Hill, but when people heard what I was actually saying, the boos turned to cheers.

stayed in touch and eventually sent him a demo tape. It was the bones of what became *The Slim Shady EP*. Paul heard that tape, and he thought it was so far beyond what I'd done on *Infinite*, you know? He got excited and went to some pay phone to call me in Detroit. He was standing outside in Manhattan, with his calling card running out, to ask if he could be my lawyer, start shopping my stuff.

I already had a manager at that time, but I would stay with Paul when I went out to New York for gigs Paul booked. We were staying at his house in Astoria, Queens, when my old manager and I wound up falling out over a Whopper sandwich. Manager dude was going to Burger King, and he didn't ask me if I wanted anything to eat, knowing I had no money. I didn't have a dollar in my fucking pocket. At that point I said, Fuck it, you know? What kind of fucking manager are you? I always thought that if you want to manage somebody, you believe in them. You invest. It's a gamble, like a roll of the dice.

The last song on the '97 demo tape was a song I never released called "Slim Shady"—but the very beginning was missing! There were three other songs on there too: "No One Iz Iller Than Me," "Low, Down, Dirty," and "Dumpin'."

After The Hip Hop Shop, I started going to bigger and bigger battles. In '97, I went to the Scribble Jam in Ohio. I got to the point where I was battling the champion— Juice. He beat me the first battle, I beat him the second. We were supposed to go to the tiebreaker. I came to find out that his manager had put together the whole event and was running the turntables. In the last round, I hit him with all my punch lines—then I choked. Juice hit me with this rhyme that he had obviously written out before—everything was structured out perfectly. He says something like, "This dude wants to stand here and act like he can drop lines / I just walk right past his ass like a stop sign." The crowd goes nuts. Juice wins the trophy. Claps all around.

I went back to Detroit depressed and totally broke. A little while after that, I started recording the original

version of a song called "Rock Bottom"—it's on *The Slim Shady LP*. It's a serious, sad song. During that session, Mark Bass and I found out that this guy who we thought was going to get us a deal at Jive Records only worked in the mail room, and he had no juice at all. I was completely depressed, in one of those just-fuck-it states. That night at the studio was the first time I ever used drugs. I swallowed a handful of Tylenol 3s. My whole mind frame was, I'm going to finish this song, and this'll be the last song I ever record. Thank God I had no tolerance for that shit, because I puked up everything in the fucking bathroom. I had to wear one of Marky's shirts home.

That's right, "honky." I used to have a sense of humor about my position in the rap world. But not anymore.

Then it was time to go to L.A. for the Rap Olympics, where I battled all these rappers and took them out. I got to the very last dude. I had metaphors stacked up. I would throw some freestyle battling in there, and then a written punch line rhyme. The whole key to freestyle is that you say a punch line that you know everyone's going to go crazy over—and because everybody's screaming they're not gonna be able to hear the next couple of lines. So you can say anything after.

In the final round, I'm supposed to be onstage going head to head, rapping face to face, man against man. But this dude named Otherwize goes behind the video screen, and he walks in the opposite direction of my rapping ass. So I've got nobody in front of me to rip apart. I don't remember any of his rhymes outside of him screaming in my face that he was gonna fuck me up, slit my throat, kill me. I don't know if anything even rhymed. "Bitch, I'll kill

you! I'll fucking drill you! I hate you! I fucking degrade you!" And that's how he beat me. The first prize was $500 and a Rolex. I don't know if the Rolex was real, but I needed money, and that $500 was real.

I was so pissed off that I had lost in the last round again. Because in Detroit, I was undefeated. It was so hard to take the loss from Juice, when I choked for the very first time, and then to choke again on somebody who wasn't anywhere near Juice's caliber at the Rap Olympics . . . I was giving up, I had lost. When I was walking away from the Rap Olympics joint, this dude Dean Geistlinger from Interscope—he worked as an assistant in Jimmy Iovine's office—walked up and asked if he could have my demo. I was in such a fucked-up mood that I just chucked a tape at him.

All I kept thinking after that was, What the fuck am I going to do? Because I was going home to nothing.

I recorded *Infinite* in 1995, my first album. It sold maybe 70 copies and didn't get great feedback. I hadn't found myself yet. A lot of people said it sounded like Nas, and he was a heavy influence at the time. But I had an album out, and I could say that. With *The Slim Shady EP*, it was a different story. That shit got some buzz in the underground, and online sites couldn't keep it in stock. I started getting calls about shows.

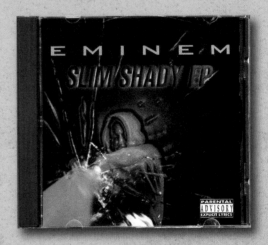

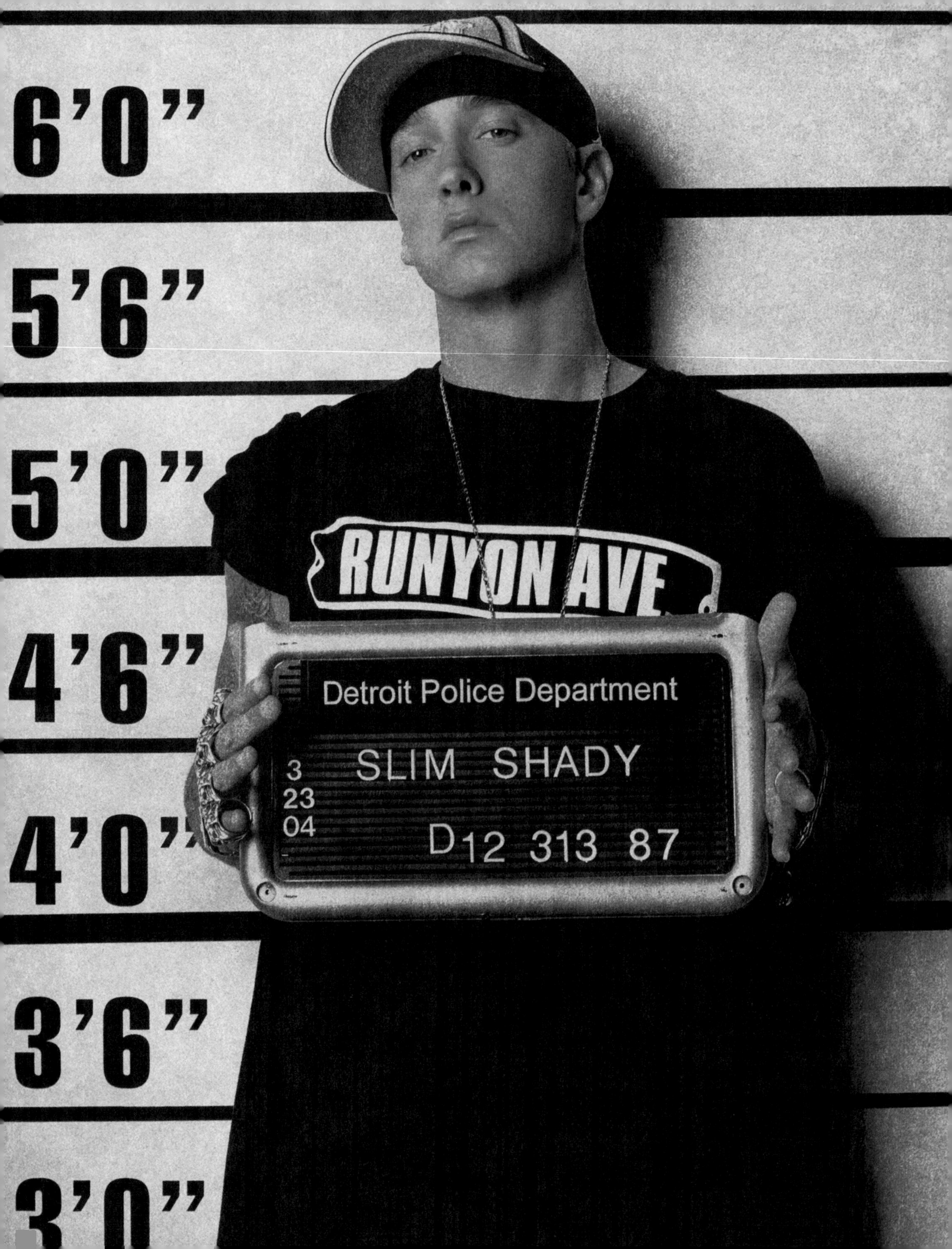
6'0"
5'6"
5'0"
4'6"
4'0"
3'6"
RUNYON AVE
Detroit Police Department
SLIM SHADY
3
23
04
D12 313 87

2

THE BIRTH, DEATH (AND RESURRECTION?) OF SLIM SHADY

I WAS LIVING IN A SHITHOLE ON FAIRPORT STREET OFF 7 MILE WHEN PROOF CALLED ME.

He said, "I want to get the 12 best emcees in Detroit and do our own version of Wu-Tang Clan." He wanted 12 emcees because he wanted to call the group the Dirty Dozen.

But we only picked six. Then Proof came up with the idea that each of us would have an alias. Each of us would have two personas, so we would each have the power of two emcees. This is one of the places where Proof played such a major part in my life, because it's where Slim Shady came from. Proof didn't give me the name, but he pushed me to come up with something real.

The name came to me when I was on the shitter. Literally. I was taking a shit and the name just hit me. You know, you do a lot of thinking when you're shitting. Whenever I sit down on the toilet, I have my pen and pad ready.

When I thought of the name Slim Shady, I started thinking of a million things to rhyme with it. And that was the turning point. I realized that this alter-ego was going to become more than just shock rap.

IT WASN'T THAT I JUST WANTED TO SHOCK PEOPLE, THERE WAS PART OF ME COMING OUT TOO. LIKE ME BEING PISSED OFF AT THE WORLD.

Looking back on the early days of my career now, when I watch myself on TV, I'm like, Why was I so fucking mad? I was mad all the time. It was kind of a joke. I felt almost like I was the Madd Rapper. (This was right when the Madd Rapper had first come out, when he did that skit on Notorious B.I.G.'s album.)

Part of it was that people had started referring to me as trailer-park trash. I went with that perception, because I felt like I did represent that . . . I mean, I was basically poor white trash. If that's what I'm going to be labeled as, then I might as well represent it to the fullest. I thought, Fuck it, I'm going to just go all out with it.

The other concept that Proof had was that all of us were supposed to rhyme about the illest, most ridiculous shit. That was originally the entire idea behind D12. Like, Bizarre used to rap about fucking pit bulls in the ass, fucking a Chihuahua, raping his grandmother . . .

We all got our style from that. We didn't take Bizarre's style—we all wanted to sound different—but we just rapped about the most shocking shit we could think of. If the average person was sitting there listening to it, they'd be like, "The fuck did he just say?"

But I didn't want to say crazy things just to say them. If I was going to do it, I had to display some lyrical skill with it too. It had to be some kind of lyrical acrobatics, syllables had to connect, and it had to make sense. In "Just Don't Give a Fuck," I say, "Don't take me for a joke, I'm no comedian." Right after I say I raped the women's swim team.

I remember the first time I performed as Shady. I did a show at a place in Detroit called The Phat House, in late '96 or '97. I was performing songs with Bizarre and Bugz, another one of the guys from D12. It was just rapping, but it was rapping with that kind of humor that was part of the Slim Shady routine. I performed "Low, Down, Dirty," "Just Don't Give a Fuck," and maybe one other song.

Slim Shady wasn't just a new type of lyrics, it was also that I delivered them in this high-pitched style. As Shady I had a whole different voice, and that's how I knew that this was going to be a whole new persona for me.

When I listen to those songs now, I'm like, Why did I rap like that? That high-pitched shit, I have no idea where it came from. It may have come from me fucking around, imitating a friend, and somehow I just started rapping like that. If you listen to my first album, *Infinite,* and then you listen to *The Slim Shady EP,* you'll notice that the two styles are completely different. I'd taken a little hiatus from recording, and

for some reason when I came back I just started rapping like that.

Once people heard Shady, they didn't want Marshall or Eminem anymore. "I've created a monster, because nobody wants to see Marshall no more. They want Shady. I'm chopped liver." I say that in "Without Me," but I'm not chopped liver. I'm the best thing that ever lived. Let's get that right, for starters. (Kidding.)

Being able to rap as an entirely different persona feels good. Proof used to describe it like this: Slim Shady is the guy who shows up after a few shots of Bacardi; Eminem is the emcee who goes onstage sober and spits his metaphors. Slim Shady gets drunk and wants to fight.

It was great to have someone else to blame. "I didn't say that, Slim Shady did." That excuse doesn't always work in real life—in real life if you live like that, people call you crazy. Rap is one big *Fantasy Island*—it's the place I always retreat to when things get too hectic in real time.

I remember seeing *Animal House* when I was a kid. I loved that flick. The thing I remember most about it was the devil-on-one-shoulder, angel-on-the-other thing. This guy is with a young girl passed out drunk, and the devil appears on his shoulder and goes, "Fuck her! Fuck her brains out." And then the angel on the other shoulder is like, "For shame! If you lay one finger on that poor, sweet, helpless girl . . ." That's sort of the relationship between Slim Shady and Eminem.

Dre understood where I was coming from with it. He was like, "What if you did a song where I'm the good guy and you're the bad guy? You're the crazy, sick fool straight out of the mental institution." Back in my younger years, I was a little more off the wall—so I was pretty much up for anything. That was the core of *The Slim Shady LP*—exploring the bad while hearing the good ring out in my head too.

When we were making the first album together, Dre had been saying, "We got the record, we just need an image." But I never thought much about what Slim Shady looked like. Then one day, I was high on E, walking the streets with Royce. We went into a drugstore and bought a bottle of peroxide. I had taken two hits of Ecstasy—I was out of my mind. The next day I looked in the mirror and I'd forgotten I'd did it. I woke up at 2 o'clock in the afternoon and was like, Holy shit! I looked like a skunk—I had no idea what I was doing with those chemicals.

When I walked back into the studio with this newly blond hair and a white T-shirt—that's all I wore back then—Dre was dead silent and just looked at me, like, Whoa, without saying it. Then I remember him saying, "That's it! We found your image!" Jimmy Iovine came up to the studio to see what Dre was raving about and he just freaked out. "This is your identity. This is the identity we've been looking for the whole time."

I WASN'T THINKING THAT THE PEROXIDE THING WAS GOING TO BE MY LOOK; I WAS JUST BEING STUPID ON DRUGS.

The line that separates Slim from Em can be really thin. Where does this Shady guy stop and Eminem come in? I think my fans can pretty much tell which one is which, to an extent.

And there's a third thing: When does Slim Shady kick in, when does Eminem step in, where does Marshall begin? Let's say "Just Don't Give a Fuck" is Slim Shady. Eminem is "Lose Yourself," and "Mockingbird" is Marshall. I think those are the most blatant, extreme examples.

I used to use Slim Shady as an excuse to rap pissed off, and I used to say that Eminem is the more lyrical rapper, more concentrated on his lyrics. And Marshall is the sincere, all-jokes-aside guy. But now I believe there's a balance to it, they're not as extreme anymore, they're not as far from each other. Slim, Em, and Marshall are all always in the mix when I'm writing now. I've found a way to morph the styles so that it's sort of all me.

We've all got Slim Shadys up inside of us: "Guess there's a Slim Shady in all of us. Fuck it, let's all stand up." There are times when every one of us can be an asshole or a smart-ass. Thing is, most responsible adults know how to ignore that dude or chick. I'm a lot better at it these days.

Slim Shady eventually became a metaphor for the trappings of fame for me. For example, in the song "When I'm Gone" I say, "Shady made me / But tonight Shady's rock-a-bye baby." And the chorus goes, "When I'm gone / Just carry on / Don't mourn / Rejoice every time you hear the sound of my voice." I was basically saying, I don't want this life anymore. I liked having Slim Shady around, but he'd become so famous that it had damn near destroyed my family.

SO I KILLED OFF SLIM SHADY.

HE'S BEEN DEAD FOR THE LAST FEW YEARS. I'VE BEEN CHILL. RAISING MY KIDS. WATCHING RAP GO TO CRAP.

My fame is still here, though. That's my reality, and there is some tragedy in that. Not that I'm looking for people to cry for me—I can cry pretty well on my own. (Slim always smacks me in the head and tells me to SHUT THE FUCK UP when I cry.)

People wonder if Shady will reemerge on my next album, even though he's supposed to be dead. Well, I suppose as long as I'm here, Shady's here.

3 SUPERNOVA

NO ONE LOOKED TWICE AT ME WHEN I FIRST GOT SIGNED TO DRE.

We would record at this studio called the Mix Room in Burbank. There was this mall nearby that I'd go to and I was just like a regular guy.

Shit got crazy fast, though—1999 was the year it all went bananas. We were doing so many shows back then, it felt like we were literally killing ourselves. And we were drinking, too. I had never really been a full-throttle drinker, but once we got on tour it was just so crazy. Sometimes we'd be waiting to perform and there would be some liquor around, and we'd just start drinking, and then next thing you know, we'd have to go onstage and perform. Afterward, we'd come offstage and drink even more excessively. Sometimes we'd do two or three shows

a day. We'd work, drink, pass out, wake up, and move on to the next show.

Any chance there was to make money, we'd take it. Sometimes, all I had to do was show my face and maybe do a song or two. Man, I remember getting $5,000 to perform one song, which was a ton back then. We were workaholics.

All I really had out was "My Name Is," and everything was still new to me. I had bleached my hair for the first time, and people started immediately associating me with that and recognizing me because of it . . . I'd be back at that same mall in Burbank—where no one had ever noticed me before—and I'd get a couple of people asking for autographs.

I fell off the stage at a concert once. I had jumped on a bike rack that was being used as a barricade, slipped, and fell. The stage was so high that I had to climb back up on the bike rack to reach it. Proof grabbed my arms and pulled me up onto the stage. I was so disoriented that I forgot which song we were on. I fell during the last verse of "Role Model," but when I got back up I forgot we had done it. So I started going, "Okay, I'm about to drown myself," and Proof laughs and says, "No you're not." And I'm like, "Yes sir, I am, I'm about to drown myself."

Airports are where things got really messed up. I flew coach until *The Marshall Mathers LP* came out. You don't know how famous you are until you're sitting in coach and people won't leave you the fuck alone and let you sleep.

After I had done MTV's Spring Break in 2000—me and Dre performed "Forgot About Dre"—I was waiting to get on a flight back home to Detroit. These two girls were sitting across from me at the gate. I'm asleep. I wake up, and I'm drooling on myself. The girls start laughing. One of them goes, "Can we see your thumbs?" And I'm like, "My thumbs?" She says, "Look at your thumbs. They bend back." I didn't even notice it until then: for some reason my thumbs hyperextend, the tip of my thumb goes back. They were fascinated by my thumbs, and they were talking about the "My Name Is" video. The other one says, "They're weird, but they're like the cutest thumbs." I've got cute thumbs. Thanks. That's great. That was weird, waking up and realizing that these girls had been staring at me the entire time. I'm not going to say I wasn't flattered a little bit. They were harmless—and cute, too. But it's one of those moments that made me wonder, Am I a freak? Am I ever going to be able to do normal things like fall asleep at the gate in a fucking airport again?

Then, during one of our tours—I can't remember which one—a plane that we were about to get on had mechanical problems, and we ended up sleeping on the floor of JFK. It's me, one of my security guys, Proof, DJ Head, a bunch of us. This young girl, maybe 16 or 17 years old, she was stuck there too, and she didn't know what to do. She was on the phone crying to her mother. Proof and I helped her out. Her parents didn't want her to get on the plane. People can get weirded out if something's wrong with the plane—they don't want to fly even after it's been fixed. I got on the phone with her parents and said, "Your little girl's going to be fine. We're going to get her to her connecting flight."

So Proof and I walked the girl to the right gate, and everything was cool. But I guess we were at that level of fame where the girl was overwhelmed that we would do something like that. She just kept thanking us over and over like what we had done was really special. But it was just the human thing to do, you know?

Proof and I came back to our little camp on the floor, and we started cracking jokes, just laughing back and forth. This army chick was sitting near us, a drill instructor or something, all camouflage and boots and shit. She said, "Hey, dickwad!" I looked over at Proof, and I'm like De Niro in *Taxi Driver*, "She talking to me? She talking to me? She's got to be talking to me, there's nobody else here."

Proof gave me the weirdest look, like, I think she's talking to you. And she said, "Yeah, you heard me, dickwad. Why don't you shut your fucking mouth, you little fucking pussy?" I didn't know what to say. Everybody in our camp just busted out laughing so hard. Then the army chick stood up like she wanted to fight me. She said, "I don't give a fuck who you are, motherfucker! Famous or not, I'll kick the fucking living shit out of you if you don't shut the fuck up!"

I didn't know whether to be afraid or keep laughing. The more I laughed and the more I smiled, the angrier she got. She started punching the wall. Just completely spazzed out. Man, I could go on forever with wack airport stories. It's like, once you're famous, people feel like they can say anything to you. Like you aren't real anymore.

Now don't get it twisted. I feel blessed. I've traveled to places that your average kid from Detroit would never go, I've had all kinds of exotic foods, and I've spent some quality time with lots of beautiful—and not so beautiful—women. But being famous is fuck-

If I had to pick a moment, I'd say the release of "My Name Is" was where all the craziness began. Dre had warned me to expect a shitstorm with *The Slim Shady LP*, but at the time I was thinking, How much of a shitstorm can it possibly be? I mean, how big am I really going to get? And even while he was warning me, he'd be egging me on. I would say the most outlandish shit, and he would laugh at it. Dre was N.W.A., you know what I'm saying? He was the king of controversy, and he loved stirring it up.

There was a point where the album was basically finished—it was mixed—and I had gone back to Detroit to take a break from recording and everything, and to see Kim and Hailie and just be with them. That was when Geffen and A&M were joining with Interscope, and I remember the Bass Brothers telling me I might need to fly back because there was talk of me getting dropped because the album was so controversial. (I was on a pay phone having this conversation because I lived in a trailer.)

There were some lines in "Role Model" and "My Name Is" that Jimmy Iovine wasn't happy with, and, well, really the whole album was causing a stir. So this merger was going on, and apparently Interscope was like, Do we really want someone this controversial? I got myself on a plane straight away, and Dre and I had this meeting with everyone—this was the meeting that's re-created in the video for "The Way I Am," where you see me getting ready to go sit at a roundtable with everybody, and I get pissed off and start throwing papers and shit like that. The real scene wasn't that dramatic, but I was trying to plead my case, you know? We're sitting down with Jimmy having this little roundtable, and I was like, "Tell me what you want me to change, because I don't understand what the big deal is. We put a parental advisory sticker on there, and I thought we were good to go, right?"

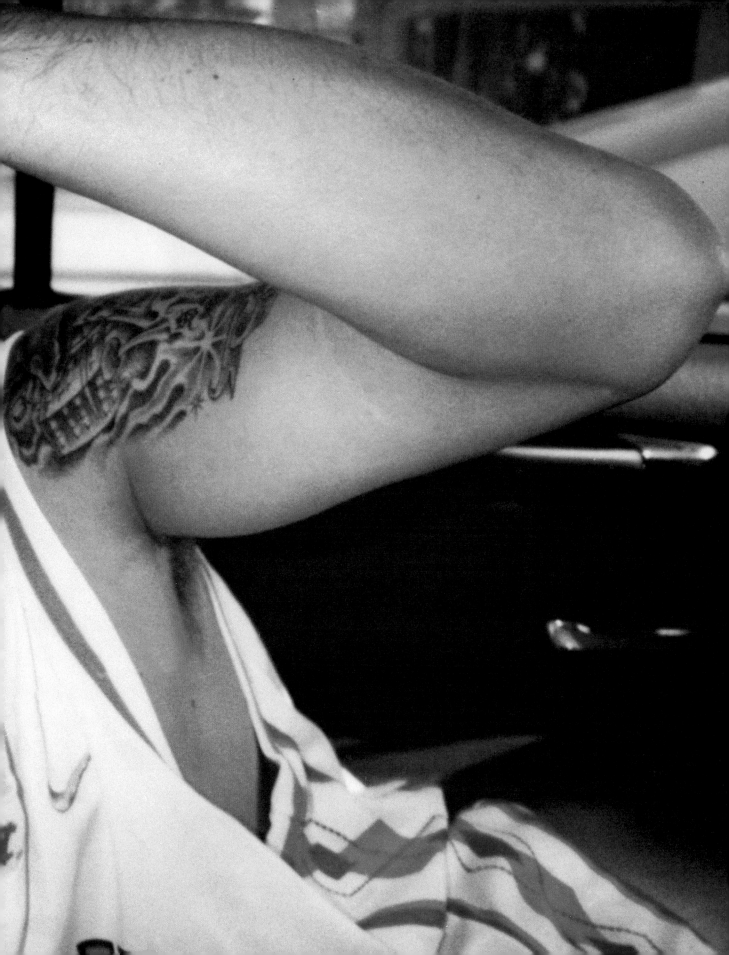

Well, another problem with that album was that the main sample interpolated in "My Name Is" was originally written by (I was told) a gay activist who'd moved to South Africa, and he was not going to let us use the song unless we changed the line, "My English teacher wanted to fuck me in junior high, only problem was my English teacher was a guy."

I ended up having to change it to "My English teacher wanted to fuck me in junior high, thanks a lot, next semester I'll be 35," but I wasn't happy about it. At first Dre and I went back to the studio and tried to create a new beat so we wouldn't have to use the guy's song, but we couldn't do it. We were sure the song was going to be a hit, so we had to make it happen. We had to have that sample. I don't make a penny off of writing on "My Name Is." Nothing. That guy owns all of the publishing on that song. But the way I justify it is I recognize,

WHAT IF THAT SONG HAD NEVER COME OUT?

WHERE WOULD I BE NOW?

So, yeah, I suppose a gay man had a hand in the explosion of Marshall Mathers. Yes! Act like you know, bros.

Changing the lines and all that was rough. I just did not get it.

Coming from where I came from, those lyrics were nothing compared to what dudes used to say to each other in battles. And what ever happened to freedom of speech? But it seemed like a small price to pay to jump-start my career.

I remember when Paul first told me that MTV added the "My Name Is" video. The first video we ever shot was "Just Don't Give a Fuck"—that was before I started bleaching my hair and shit—but they wouldn't take it, for pretty obvious reasons. When Paul told me they took "My Name Is," we were in his little office in New York, and they played it that day. I saw it for the very first time on the TV at his office, then we went back to his apartment and played it again, and it's really fucking hard to describe, but I had this feeling of disbelief.

I think I first started realizing how seriously people were taking me when *The Slim Shady LP* came out, and Kurt Loder and MTV got wind of the original lyrics of "My Name Is." That was sort of the start of the whole gay controversy. I was just like, "Come on, it was supposed to be funny, just a joke."

It was a bitter pill to swallow. I remember feeling so boxed in, like I really had to watch everything I say. I got tired of explaining myself, so with *The Marshall Mathers LP*, I just went into the "faggot" zone. Like on purpose. Like, Fuck you.

Even then I didn't believe everything was for real. It was hard enough to realize that I was famous enough that people gave a shit what I said, and even harder to believe that they'd take it all so fucking seriously. But even with all the hate, my fan base was getting bigger and bigger. I think I finally felt the real heat of my success when *The Marshall Mathers LP* hit middle America. It sold 1.76 million in the first week.

"The Real Slim Shady" was my biggest hit then, and the 2000 VMAs were a real milestone. I can't front, I was nervous about that performance. When I saw all those look-alikes walking out of Radio City Music Hall, I was trying to be as cool as I could and keep my composure, but for at least the first 30 seconds of the song I could not shake my nerves off. I watched a DVD of that night recently, and I can see how tense I was. Live TV performances are a funny thing: if you fuck up, you fuck up in front of millions of people. And you don't get a chance to

go back and fix it. That was one of those moments when I was thinking, Hey, I think I've made it in rap. I'm a big-time rapper, rappin' big-time! That's the only way to go to an awards show, if you ask me: a hundred deep with dudes who look like you and who can hopefully fight like you. They didn't end up needing to, of course, but still . . . I hope they got laid. The response I received after that awards show performance was crazy. I think it helped people realize that I was here for real, that I wasn't playin'.

I haven't always been into awards shows.

I DIDN'T START RAPPING FOR TROPHIES.

The trophies I was after weren't sculpted little men. I just wanted my respect around the way, you know?

The first year that I was nominated for a Grammy, I didn't even go to the ceremony. There was this separation between the Best Album category and the Best Rap Album category, and I didn't understand it. Why not just Best Album? Why separate rap music? I ended up winning two Grammys that year, but it still didn't make sense to me. At that time, fame was so new to me, and I was thinking, Who even votes on this? I'm not going to this shit. I'd rather go to MTV or BET and get an award there—because it's coming from the fans who are actually buying records. I finally went in 2001, because, come on, how ridiculous was it that I kept winning and not being there? Like, what kind of asshole am I? At a certain point, yes, I have to respect the people in the industry who respect me and my craft. Time to grow up, Marshall.

My performance with Elton John that year—that was history right there. He was so cool to me; he really got where I was coming from and he knew that I wasn't this straight-up homophobic dude. Elton put himself at risk by performing with me—in terms of alienating his fans who had a problem with me—and I'll always respect him for that. The gesture helped immensely, and it made me not sweat the fact that there were all those protesters outside wanting me to go away forever. They gave me three Grammys that year—even with all the controversy. I'm so GLAAD that we've moved on from the situation N.O.W.

BELIEVE IT OR NOT, IT WAS MY IDEA TO PERFORM WITH ELTON. I WAS THINKING, WHAT WOULD REALLY SHOCK PEOPLE AND ULTIMATELY BRING THEM TOGETHER?

Elton and me—we're friends. He got married to another man! He's gay! And we're friends! And who cares? At our rehearsal for the Grammys, he went off about the people who were against me. I think it's hard for some people to understand that for me the word "faggot" has nothing to do with sexual preference. I meant something more like assholes or dickheads. When people got all up in arms about it, I started to use it more just to piss them off even worse. But I'm not in a position to really comment on this stuff because I'm not gay, and, ultimately, who you choose to be in a relationship with and what you do in your bedroom is your business.

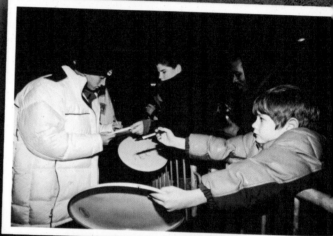

I hooked up with The Roots for the 2003 Grammys to do "Lose Yourself." They are my favorite full-band rap group and I respect those guys so much. Their music is dead on. Their timing as a group is perfect. At that point it felt like I was at the height of my fame, and whatever I could do to open the eyes of people, to widen their idea of what hip-hop was, I wanted to do. When I got together with The Roots for rehearsal, it was like fucking magic. That performance turned out really dope and was a fun, great experience.

When my popularity grew to middle America, some people started to compare me to Elvis. Is he stealing black music and culture? That was the last thing I was trying to do. I was just doing the music that I grew up on and that I love.

THAT WAS JUST A CRAZY TIME. I COULDN'T GO ANYWHERE WITHOUT GETTING MOBBED.

I tried to remember what it was like to be a fan, and I signed as many autographs as I could. I used to try to do something different with each autograph I signed, but then the stacks got bigger and bigger, and it got hard to keep it original. And then I started to write stuff like "Stay cool!" "Stay up!" For a girl, I'd write stuff like "Stay sweet!" I was always happy to sign them, though. I was still at a point where it was like, I can't even believe I'm doing this.

I thought *The Marshall Mathers LP* was as crazy as it was going to get. In my mind, I was feeling like, I've peaked. I've already peaked on my second album. Okay, on my third album things are going to have to start winding down. But then I sold just as many on the next record. I didn't know how to call it. Just when I expected things to slow down, the pace just stayed the same or maybe even got crazier.

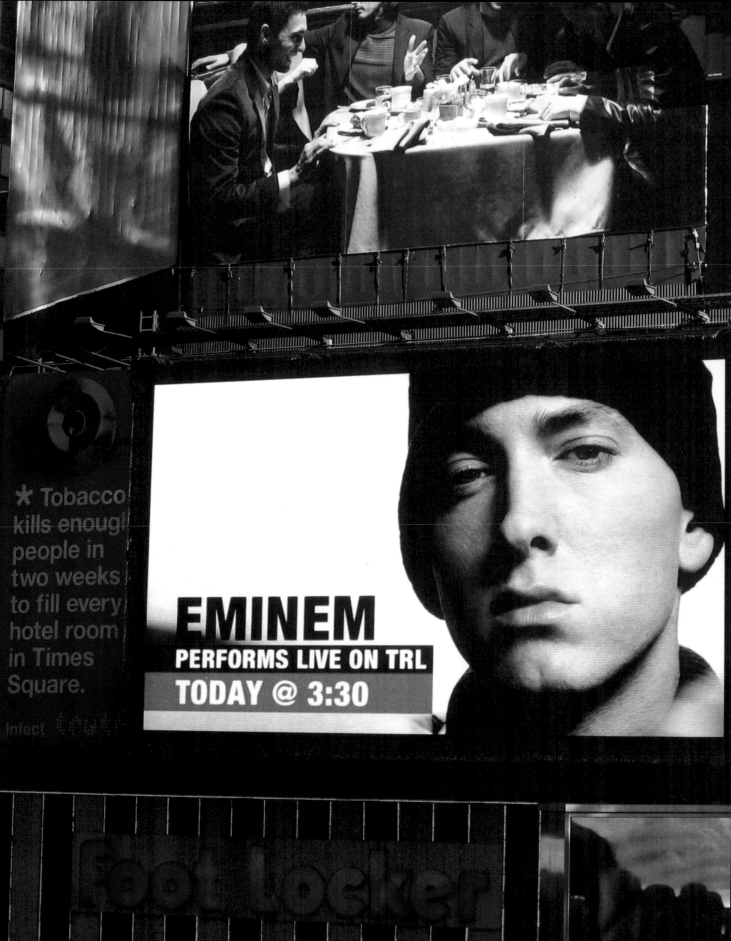

BIG PROOF AIR MAX 1

SHADE 45 AIR MAX 180

AIR JORDAN IV RETRO EMINEM ENCORE

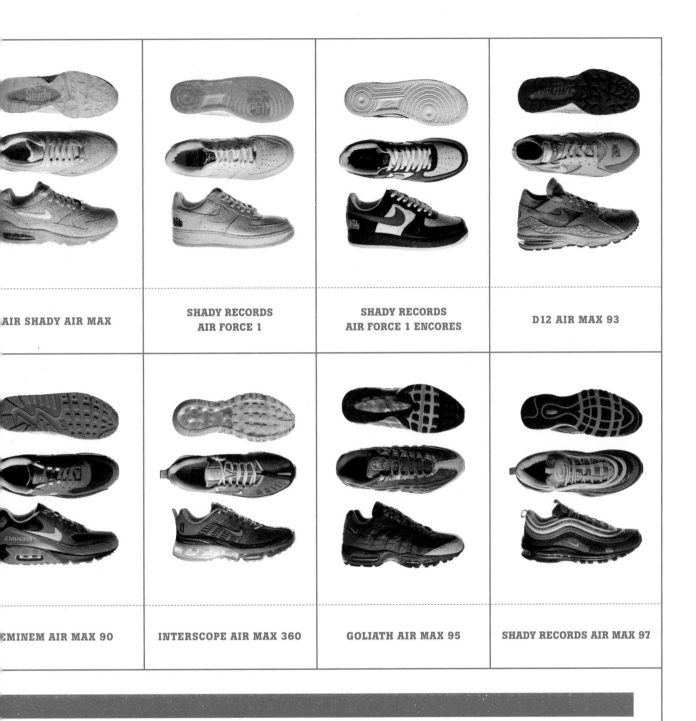

AIR SHADY AIR MAX

**SHADY RECORDS
AIR FORCE 1**

**SHADY RECORDS
AIR FORCE 1 ENCORES**

D12 AIR MAX 93

EMINEM AIR MAX 90

INTERSCOPE AIR MAX 360

GOLIATH AIR MAX 95

SHADY RECORDS AIR MAX 97

Being a celebrity has one perk that I'm not ashamed to name: limited-edition sneakers. If you'd told me back in the day that there'd be Shady or D12 kicks, I'd have laughed at you. These Nikes are all dope, especially the Air Jordan IV's that have been nicknamed "Blueberries"—there are only 50 pairs in the world. We made them and the Shady Records Air Force 1 Encores when I put out the *Encore* album. The first shoe we ever did with Nike was the Air Shady Air Max—I still wear those kicks. The Shady Records Air Force 1s are pretty rare too. Under the gel on the bottom is the signature of every artist on the Shady label at that time. The rest of these are part of a nine-pair Air Max line we did with Nike to raise money for their Nine Million charity. I've always wanted to be able to design shoes like this anyway, so it's really special to do so while helping people at the same time.

I was getting free shit thrown at me: clothes, booze, harder stuff, women. Hamburgers. I'm just a regular dude from Detroit, though. I've maintained that relationship with my hometown for many years because I'm a loyal dude. The road could have been really crazy for me—and it was—but my party was mostly the substances. The funny thing is,

I DIDN'T REALLY START DOING DRUGS UNTIL I RAPPED ABOUT THEM.

When I was younger, I'd drink a 40 after work or maybe smoke a little weed. I had friends who experimented with mushrooms and shit like that, but I wouldn't do it. When you're on tour, though, it's just a whole different world.

The first time I went to Amsterdam was for the promotion of the *The Slim Shady LP*. Man, we were young. I was probably 27. Going there for the first time was a crazy experience. It just seemed liked everyone was doing drugs—all the time, everywhere.

I couldn't get over how everyone was so free about it. I referenced that in my music, and we even thought about calling the second album *Amsterdam* because of that trip.

After that, when I was on tour rapping about Vicodin, or mushrooms, or Ecstasy, people started throwing that shit my way. It was just one of those things—wherever we went, people would be like, "Hey man, we got some Ecstasy." Or, "We got some mushrooms." I couldn't believe the effect my lyrics had on people—they thought we were literally drug addicts and that they could get backstage or whatever by bringing us some substances. It was wild. I was never walking around with E in my own pocket, but if someone had it and they offered it, it was like, Okay, cool, join the crowd. Welcome to rock and roll.

This one time in Texas, Proof and I took some mushrooms some dude had given to us the day before. We had a show that night at 8 o'clock, and we didn't want to take them too late in the day because they're extremely hard to come down from, so we took them around noon. There was a courtyard in the middle of the hotel, and we went down there and started throwing around this Nerf football, but it just kept smacking us in the face because our depth perception had gone completely fucking haywire. So we're throwing the ball, and we're laughing, and we think it's hilarious. At some point we must have gone back into the room, because I remember he was on one bed, and I was on the other, and we were jumping up and down like little fucking kids. Next thing you know, we sort of crashed and we're hanging off the beds, right? And we're looking at each other, and we're upside down. I looked over at Proof and said, "Are you coming down yet?" And he laughed and said, "No, are you?" I said, "Fuck, what are we gonna do? Our show is in an hour and a half." . . . There's no big ending to that story. Sorry. That memory just sticks out for me. Probably because it was just Proof and me, goofing around like idiots.

As people know, the whole drug thing built into a problem for me at some point. I'm glad that I realized it and set myself in the right direction, trying to do something about it. It was dumb to even get started, but being young and dumb went hand in hand for me. I've had good people around me the whole time to help me through it— my Shady family. We're pretty tight.

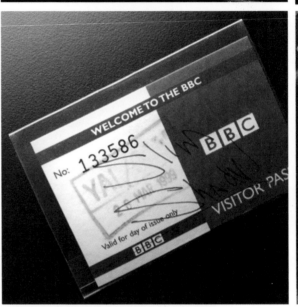

For obvious reasons, I've forgotten a lot of the small stuff, a lot of the details about the road, but I'll never forget what it's like to be in front of a wild crowd. There's nothing like a hype live show. Nothing beats it.

I remember my first sold-out show like it was yesterday. It was at Tramp's in New York City in January of '98. MTV was there, and I was performing with Royce da 5'9". I was downstairs in the dressing room when Paul came down and said we'd sold out, and that there were people literally squeezing through the doors trying to get in. I was like, "Holy shit! Holy shit!" I was just "holy shitting" it through that whole

night, and all I could think was, I cannot believe this is happening. After that show, MTV interviewed me. I think that was my first TV interview ever.

Other shows, man, I've seen people in the front row, saying the whole shit, every lyric to every song. I'm looking at them like, Goddamn, they know the words better than I do! When I fuck up, they know the words and shit—fill in the blanks. That's crazy. There were shows where the people were so loud that we couldn't rap for 10 minutes. I remember this show in Oslo where the crowd went nuts, and I just felt like my life was a dream that was so good that I would wake up from it, realize that my real life sucked, then not know how to handle the harsh reality.

The Sober Tour, AKA Anger Management Europe. I remember asking Proof, "Hey, what ever happened to the days when we used to just go out and rock the crowd?" Because for a while I was doing shows where I didn't even see the people. I was just looking out into space. On this particular tour, my eyes aren't bulged out, and I'm slapping hands and connecting with people. I'd come to realize that we weren't going to get booed, people had paid to come see us perform. So we actually didn't have to worry about getting hammered right before we went out onstage anymore. There wasn't anything to fear. On this tour, it was time to take control.

No offense to the United States, but European crowds—because they don't always get acts from the United States—they go *nuts*. It's like it's a special thing for them. Man, I appreciate it. I've played in front of like 70,000 people over there. And when you get that many people in a stadium, it's time to mess with the in-ear monitors—it's the only way I can hear. In situations like that, I can't even tell how that many people can hear the fucking music. Especially the people in the nosebleed seats.

One of my best show memories was The Slim Shady Tour at the House of Blues in Los Angeles. Backstage, between the first and second back-to-back shows that night, I met Dustin Hoffman and his kids. I was really excited to meet the original Rain Man, and he started asking who wore the mummy suit we were using as a cheap gag prop at the time. Then—I think to impress his kids—he asked whether he could *be* the mummy in the next show. He did it and revealed himself at the end, and the crowd went nuts. Dustin Hoffman, back then, bringing his white family to a rap show . . . Honestly, I'd love to be remembered as one of the best to ever pick up a mic, but if I'm doing my part to lessen some racial tension I feel good about what I'm doing.

I WANT TO BRING PEOPLE TOGETHER.

I FEEL LIKE THAT CAN BE MY BIGGEST CONTRIBUTION TO HIP-HOP.

4

VERY FUNNY, MOTHERFUCKER

EVEN BEFORE I STARTED RAPPING, I WAS

SNAPPING ON PEOPLE.

This was back in junior high and high school. Well, 8th grade and those three real *precious* years I spent in 9th grade. I had to choose between being the class clown and being the shy kid who got the shit kicked out of him. So whenever I had a choice, it was pretty much guaranteed I was going to act the fool and start clowning. But, you know, usually you don't get to make that choice.

When I was nine years old, this kid who was a little older decided one day to just beat the living shit out of me in the bathroom at elementary school. Almost killed me. I rapped about that in "Brain Damage," and some people think I'm making it up, but nope—that shit really happened. My brain really was fucking bleeding out my ear. It wasn't like I was in a coma, but I was kind of blacking out and waking up off and on for a couple of days. When I finally came out of it, my first words were "I can spell elephant." I guess I felt like a Ringling Brother.

So I had to learn quickly to snap back. And, luckily, snapping on people and being snapped on is something that kind of trains you for hip-hop. It's a lot like battling. You have to be sharp: if you don't have a comeback ready or if you blurt out something weak or just not funny, you're going to sound like an ass. A lot of really great hip-hop is just a hot beat and guys coming up with amazing disses.

I should be grateful. If I hadn't gotten the shit kicked out of me, I might never have started snapping, and then I might never have started rapping. I'd probably still be cooking at Gilbert's Lodge for $5.50 an hour. I mean, I basically was working there when I first met Dre. Hailie at that time was just a baby, about a year old. Do you know how many hours it takes working as a cook to earn enough money to buy a box of diapers? Four or five hours. So in the end I guess I'm not so mad about the brain damage.

I think maybe there's this perception out there that I'm still this withdrawn, quiet guy, and that the clowning around I do in my music is a way to get around being shy. But I'm really just a normal guy. You can ask my neighbors. I ride a bike. I walk the dog. I mow my lawn. I'm out there every Sunday, talking to myself, buck naked, mowing the lawn with a chainsaw.

The press probably gets this impression of me because in interviews I'm not always bouncing around in a fucking costume, doing voices, and acting goofy. But who the fuck is going to be cracking jokes after being asked the same damn questions for the 10th year in a row? And then when you do finally say something offhand, kind of clowning around, that's the only part of the interview they end up printing. "Every morning I suck elephant cock." Then the next month you pick up the magazine and on the front cover in big letters is "Eminem: Elephant Cock Sucker!" That's a bad example, though, because, you know, every morning I do suck elephant cock. Right after I floss.

HOLY TITS!

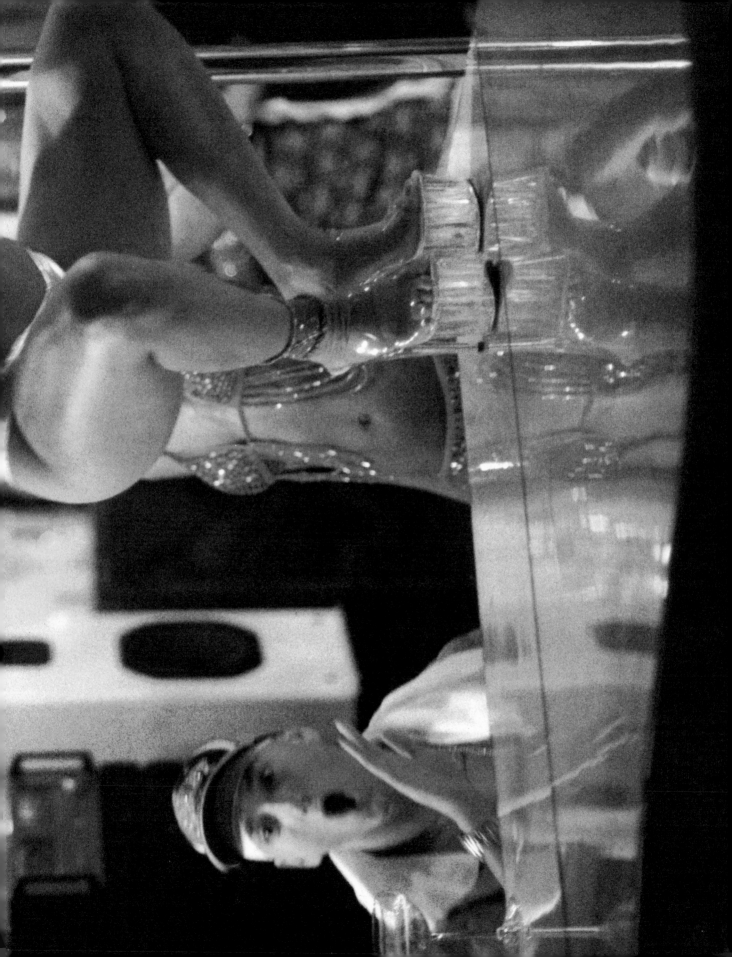

ANYWAY, I'VE ALWAYS BEEN KIND OF A PRANKSTER.

When my uncle Ronnie and I were growing up together, we used to do prank calls all the time. We would just call up random numbers and say something like, "This is your doctor. I'm afraid you have herpes." Or, "This is the fire department. Your house is on fire." You're pregnant, you're going to die, whatever. We were basically trying to be as fucked up as we could be, to try to keep people on the phone as long as we could. It didn't really work. We'd come out with something like, "You need to stick your fist up your ass," and they would just hang up.

SO PRANK CALLING IS SOMETHING I'VE BEEN DOING FOR—DECADES.

When I first saw the show *Crank Yankers*, I thought, I've got to do this. I've still got that kind of fucking 6th-grade humor in me, and the show definitely taps into that. And

I mean that as a sincere compliment. I think most people who worked with *Crank Yankers*, the producers probably called them up and asked them to do it. Not me. I called *Crank Yankers*.

And of course I've incorporated lots of phone calls into my albums. I think a lot of those calls may actually have been funnier because they were done on my own terms. I like to do skits like these because some of my songs, well, they're dark. I don't want to record 13 or 14 tracks like that in a row—I'd probably flip out and kill someone. Also, you don't want to just keep hitting people over the head with dark songs. Sometimes you can get people's attention and hold it longer if you put in lighter things like little skits and interludes. Sprinkle in some shit that's funny, so when it's time to be serious again people can give their full, undivided attention to the misogyny and the drugs and the descriptions of the corpses.

Basically, the way *Crank Yankers* worked is that the producers would come up with the basis for the call, like, "You're a guy who keeps passing the phone over to your brother, so you two keep asking the same questions over and over," and then the rest is all pretty much freestyle. We did something like 20 or 30 calls, and they ended up using three on the show. Which was fine with me because I still had a good time pranking those other 27 people.

When I'm hanging with D12, I'm always ribbing on everybody, impersonating them and shit like that. We actually all do it to each other, but I think I do it more than others. To be honest, I need to do it just to get the rest of the business out of my head. When I'm recording an album, I'm in the studio full-time. I live there. And you can go crazy in a recording booth. I mean, you're basically just a dude sitting alone in a padded room babbling to yourself and playing with a drum machine for days on end. So when I get out I'm constantly snappin' on people just to keep my mind straight. They probably don't see it that way, though.

On the routine from *Encore* where I phone up Paul, I wanted to make him have to hear the sound of my turds dropping in a toilet. Because this is what I expect my crew to do for me: listen to and compliment me on the sound of my beautiful, perfectly formed turds. So I took the mic in the bathroom and I actually shit on it. Well, not right on microphone, but I had it right there in the bowl so it could pick up the sound. It's fucked up, but it was probably one of the funniest things I've ever done. Gross, right?

Most of the funny stuff I've done has involved imitating people. I've been a mimic since back in junior high. I think it seeped into my music because of the time I spent working with the guys in D12. A lot of the dudes in D12 have an extreme sense of humor. You spend time with them, and if you don't already have that twisted humor in you, you'll pick it up. They were my gateway drug.

I'm always doing accents when I'm with my Shady peoples. I think I do a pretty funny British accent—which is nice because it's one of the few accents that shouldn't piss anybody off, right, because, you know, who has beef with England? I can do kind of offensive accents, too. I do an okay Middle Eastern cab driver—I drove Kurt Loder around Detroit using that accent for an interview back in 1999. And of course I do the horny, drug-addicted, homophobic dirtball—AKA my normal voice.

The Ken Kaniff character, which I've used on a couple albums and in a few concerts, also sort of came out of real life. There's a place in Detroit called Caniff Street, and I remember, for some reason, driving under an overpass and just trying to string together words that begin with the same letter. For example, a bunch of *L*s, like lazy, lackluster, ludicrous . . . you know.

When I started doing that I remembered Caniff, and then, I don't know why, that led to "Ken Kaniff," my gay friend from . . . well, at that point I had no idea where he was from. Then I said, "Made a couple of crank calls collect," because that's what I wanted to do on the song "Cum On Everybody." And then I wanted to keep the *K* sound going. "Made a couple of crank calls collect [to] Ken Kaniff from Connecticut, can you accept?" And once I did that, he became a character. Other people, I guess they think about serious things when they're driving. I just fuck around with the alphabet.

Paul's my manager, and he's basically paid to make sure I don't get busted with a gun again. He's a chill guy—we've been working together for 13 years, and I don't know how many people know this but he can actually rhyme. But you always have to remember that the dude's a lawyer. He went to fucking law school. When you hear that worried part of him, the lawyer's nerves, coming out in his messages, it's hilarious. And, you know, Paul is always fucking with me about guns. That's partly why I fucked with him back. I don't have a gun, but in the skit from *Encore* you can hear a gun cracking and a bullet falling out. I guess I was trying to be funny. I don't know if it worked.

If I touch on a subject in a song and it has the potential to be funny, we're probably going to figure out a way to base some video around it. With "My Name Is," I remember Dre saying, "You know, it'd be crazy if you dressed up like Marilyn Manson." And at that time, I hadn't really seen too many videos of Marilyn Manson. His reputation was fucked up in middle America, but when I mentioned him I suddenly thought, Wait a minute, I better actually look at some videos, because I don't know exactly how this guy acts. After I saw some clips of him I had a good idea of what I wanted to do. A Marilyn Manson imitation actually comes pretty naturally when you're wearing a vinyl jumpsuit and tons of white make-up. Doing Madonna, which I did in "Just Lose It," is the same: put on some cone tits and a blond wig and you can motherfucking vogue.

Bizzarre on stage as "the new lead singer!" At rehearsal

Kuniva . . . or -- Chicken bucket head!

KUNIVA, BIZZARRE & KON ARTIST

Denaun & Kuniva in 1996, exept, in 96, Denaun had a neck!!

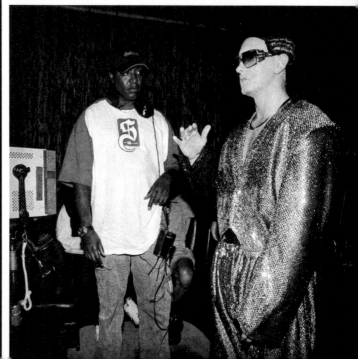

We come up with a lot of the funny stuff in the videos on the spot. We'll get a basic treatment, and then when we're on the set someone will say, "What if we tried this?" "What if we set up the camera to do this?" When we were shooting "Without Me," I came out of the dressing room as Rap Boy, with this big bunch of socks in my thing. You watch enough cartoons as a kid, you realize pretty quick that those guys are cruising around in their underpants. I told the director, Joseph Kahn, to set up the camera in the car, real low at my feet so I could rap from behind the huge bulge. It's so big I have to lean out over it. In the

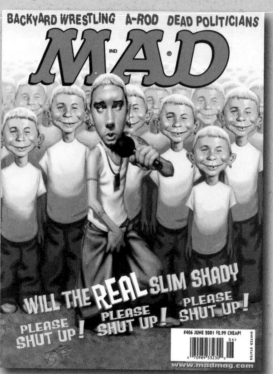

same video, I'm trying to get up off the pot and I just start break dancing as Elvis. I could barely move in that fucking big-ass prosthetic suit. But I wanted to break dance anyway, just to do the little moves I'd learned and shit.

I've been joking long enough that I don't get all fucked up when the jokes are on me. I mean, I try not to take them too seriously. I think I've grown up a lot over the years. I've cleaned up my act. And most importantly, my dick is now just ridiculously huge. I think I've probably added an inch, maybe two inches in either direction these past couple years. Ladies (and gentlemen), you've been warned.

At this point, I just try to take everything in stride. Honestly, as long as nobody says anything stupid about my daughters, who I firmly believe should be off-limits, I'm good. And if anyone's going to talk about raping my mother or hacking up Kim's body, it's going to be me. We keep that shit in the family.

I think one of the things I like to do in my songs—like in "My Name Is," for example—is take the piss out of myself before anyone goes at me. After that song, suckers knew that pretty much nothing they could say was going to hurt me. They couldn't say anything about me that I hadn't already said. In 8 Mile, Jimmy's whole strategy is to take whatever someone's going to say about him and use it against them. That's been my strategy as a rapper.

And when they do slip through, when somebody does manage to crack jokes on you, you just have to laugh with them. When they first put me on the cover of Mad magazine—I think I've been on the cover four times—I hung the issue up in my basement. The way I see it, you know you've made it when you're in Mad magazine.

Weird Al also got at me. He made a video, did a fake interview with me, spliced it with clips from my old interviews, and put it up on the Internet. He's a very funny motherfucker. When something like that happens you have to sit back and say, "Oh, he got me." It's something you pick up from battles: you learn to be a good sport about a lot of stuff. If you want to dish it out, you've got to be able to take it. I used to wash dishes. I used to have dishpan hands. So what?

This is especially true for the people I'm closest to. Like Denaun from D12—AKA Mr. Porter. We've been working together for a while now, but we were also roommates for a couple years. If you're roommates with somebody and you're also working with him, it's going to start. There's no holding back. We'd say to Denaun, "Denaun Porter, you've got a deer leg," because, well, he got shot in his leg. Actually, Von—AKA Kuniva—started the whole deer leg thing: "Shut the fuck up, deer leg." And he'd say there were flies flying around Denaun's leg, and maggots and stuff. So we used to do this ritual before we'd go onstage, after we did the prayer, where we'd get in a circle and Denaun would put his deer leg in the center, and we would all do a little motion with our hands, and we'd make buzzing sounds as if there were flies flying around his deer leg.

That kind of snapping on each other is always going both ways when I'm with my crew. Everyone gets it, even me. And what do people say about me? That I'm great. How incredible I am. That I'm a fucking genius. That I have beautiful, perfectly formed turds. Stuff like that. Act like you know, ho.

NO, THE NUMBER 2 COMES WITH ONION RINGS, NOT FRIES

HOW MANY BLONDE WHITE BOYS

DOES IT TAKE TO MAKE A VIDEO?

UH OH, BABY-MAMA DISPUTE

SO DO I RAP NOW, OR DOES SHE SING?

NAP TIME

WHERE THE SNORES THUNDER

AND THE DROOL FLOWS FREE

WILL YOU PLEASE FUCK OFF FOR 2 MINUTES SO I CAN SLEEP?

ANY TIME, ANYWHERE

EVERYONE'S FAVORITE FINGER

JESUS CHRIST, PROOF,
HOW MANY TIMES I GOTTA TELL YOU?
THAT'S THE WRONG FINGER!

BIZARRE, I JUST NEED THIS MUCH
COOPERATION FROM YOU, OK?

OKAY, WHERE'S THE DAMN TOILET?

WHAT, NO CHEESE WITH MY WINE?   I'M GOIN' HOME

PROOF IS HOLLERIN' AT THE BITCHES, AS USUAL

NO BREAKS?
I CAN SLEEP STANDING, DAMMIT

JUST

WRONG

SOMEONE PLEASE CALL SECURITY

DON'T CALL HIM MINI-EM,

HIS NAME'S VERNE, DAMMIT!

5 EIGHT MILE

Ever since *The Marshall Mathers LP* came out, I'd wanted to do a movie showing something similar to how I came up, something loosely based on that part of my life. I always believed that a lot of kids would be able to relate to my story, the story of the underdog.

THE UNDERDOG WHO WINS.

Back in 2000, people were offering me roles in films, coming at me with movie offers and stuff. It was something I knew I might want to dabble in at some point, but I wanted to stay focused on the music for the time being and do films later. I did kind of worry about making a film: I felt like it was going to affect my recording by taking me out of the studio—which is where I really wanted to be. And also, what if you take all this time to do a movie and then it fails?

What kept me interested was that I knew I wanted to do something authentic, and something that had a reason for being out there—I didn't want to just bank on my success.

Then Jimmy Iovine set up a meeting with this guy Brian Grazer, who ended up being one of the producers of my film. For the first half of our first meeting I was kind of sitting back and just feeling him out. Brian said he'd seen me on MTV—"EM TV" in particular, which was a special deal where I kind of took over for a bit and was all over the network. He said that seeing me in that light made him want to work on something with me. He saw that I had potential as an actor. Then he started asking me about my music, and how much of it came out of the reality of my life. I could tell he wanted to make something real, something that would speak to me and the kids out there like me. So the meeting ended, and we said we'd pick a writer, work out some ideas, and go from there.

Sure, I worried about the acting part of it. It wasn't my world. But Ice Cube dropped some science on me once. He told me that anybody who raps should be able to act. And that's not to say that what any of us rap about is phony, but, for instance, if you've got a song where you're really pissed off, and you're laying down the vocals and then for some reason you've got to redo some lines, you've got to put that same aggression out there again. It has to match what you've already recorded, as far as intensity. Which is just like acting out a scene in a movie. Or if something that you're acting out mirrors something you went through in real life, you have to reenact that experience in a way that makes it believable.

Your first time acting, things can be uncomfortable. You don't really know the actors you're working with, and then all of a sudden you have to act really pissed off about something for the movie. You think "pissed off" and you get pissed off, and then, okay, now you have to push this guy, and he has to push you back. Before we started filming I worked with an acting coach for a couple of sessions. It all went down in my basement. The simplest way to describe my "theatrical" education is: I was taught how to say the same thing in lots of different ways. Simple, but it really worked.

IT WAS SO CLOSE TO THAT PERIOD OF MY LIFE IT WAS CRAZY.

When the first version of the script came along, I remember thinking it was so close to that period of my life it was crazy. I knew it was the story I wanted to do. It took me a while to finally start reading it—because I can't stand reading. I mean, if there are no pictures in a book, forget it. The only book that I can remember ever reading front to back was LL Cool J's, and that was when I was on planes a lot. (If you're a fan of LL, and you want to know some really personal things about him, it's a pretty good fucking book.) But anyway, once I started reading that script and got past the first three, four, five pages, I was completely drawn into it. I called Paul and said, "Let's do it." Proof and I had sat down with the scriptwriter, Scott Silver, and told him a bunch of crazy stories. We told him how we used to battle, told him about the clubs we used to go to, and the script started to come together even more.

At the same time, a lot of this role was so close to me as a person that it felt natural. I'm not trying to be egotistical, but I kind of thought, I got this. It's not like someone was asking me to play a cop—you know, someone completely different from who I am. In the movie, I play a guy named Jimmy who grows up in Detroit and is trying to make it as a rapper, and the whole thing takes place in '95—when I was in Detroit trying to make it as a rapper. It really took me back to the time before I was famous.

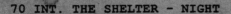

70 INT. THE SHELTER - NIGHT   70

    Jimmy walks down the long corridor to the stage. Walking
    tall. Comfortable. Focused. Ready.

    He walks on stage. Under the toxic glare of the lights.
    People crowded along the edges.
    LC Lyckety-Splyt's already there, standing next to Future.
    Shit-eating grin on his skinny little face.

    We see the crowd from Jimmy's point of view. It's a mob
    scene. Rowdy. Overflowing. Electric. Some of them boo.
    Sol is subdued. DJ Iz looks worried. Even Chedder Bob looks
    scared. Jimmy spots Alex, by herself. Seeing him, she nods.
    He nods back, acknowledging. He's here.
    People get ready.
    Jimmy sees Wink (white bandage over his nose), hanging out
    with Papa Doc, Lotto, & Moochie. Everybody looking at <u>him</u>.

    Future introduces Lyckety-Splyt.
    He's going first.
    The DJ lays down a beat.

    And LC Lyckety-Splyt's all over Jimmy.

    <u>Freestylin' about</u>--
    1. Jimmy's failure in the last battle.
    2. Jimmy being white.
    3. Jimmy's black eye.

    Jimmy just bobs his head to the beat, looking down, not
    reacting to a thing Lyckety-Splyt spits.

    Time. The crowd shouts, cheers.
    Lyckety-Splyt laughs.

    It's now Jimmy's turn. All the lights are on him. Blinding.
    The Future introduces him, hands him the mic.
    Some people start booing.
    Yell shit at him.
    Judging Jimmy.

    Jimmy bounces, collecting his thoughts, tuning out the world.
    Not hearing it. This is it. It's just him. And the beat.

    Beat.

    And Jimmy just goes off--
    All the anger pouring out of every muscle in his body.
    Into this moment. Forgetting about his pain.
    Spitting fire.

For a while the script was labeled "Untitled Detroit Project." I was the one who had the idea to call it *8 Mile*. The director, Curtis Hanson, and I have argued about this. (It's a friendly argument.) He says that he came up with the title. My take is: Curtis, no offense, but you live in L.A., and you didn't even know what 8 Mile was until you came here to Detroit and I showed you around.

IN DETROIT, 8 MILE ROAD IS THE BORDER BETWEEN THE BLACK AND THE WHITE NEIGHBORHOODS.

Both sides of 8 Mile Road are poor, but there's a definite dividing line between the black and white sides. And that's where the name of the film came from. That barrier we face.

The studio didn't want to do it, but I insisted on shooting in Detroit, which is where I shoot a lot of videos and things like that. If I can help in any way to create jobs there I'm all for it. Detroit has been in a shitty financial state for far too long.

8 MILE CLEANERS

HOT TAMALES
ROCKS TOPLESS

Hot Tamalés

8 MARKET
8065
OPEN
Welcome

BEER·WINE
SUPER 8 FOOD M
8621
FRESH MEAT · PRODUCE
BEER&WINE·DELI COUNTER
GROCERIES·FOOD STAMPS
OPEN 7 DAY

BOTTOMS UP PARTY STORE
LIQUOR
BEER·WINE·CHECK CASHING
SUPER LOTTO M$L Daily
MoneyGram

It was great to be home, but still, filming *8 Mile* was a real grind. I had a trailer where I'd hang out with my daughters. Then, when it was time to get into wardrobe again, the nanny would step in. I'd make sure the girls had coloring books, crayons, and whatever they wanted to keep them entertained until it was time for me to come back. Once the kids left the set I would go over to another trailer and run on the treadmill. Then I'd go over to the studio trailer and lay some vocals down—I was sitting there writing "Lose Yourself"

and "8 Mile" in between shooting scenes and taking care of my kids.

That whole time, whenever I wasn't rehearsing my lines I was writing lyrics. I kept a pen in my hand, and it got to the point where they would say "Action!" and I'd have to hand the pen and pad over to somebody before I went to shoot the scene. Since doing this movie took me back to before I was known by anybody, it kind of stripped me of my ego. I had to capture that, go back to that.

THE RAP BATTLE SCENES WERE

INTENSE.

FILMING THEM ACTUALLY FELT LIKE BEING IN A CLUB.

I was having some serious flashbacks. When I used to go at it with other emcees, I was never really thinking about theatrics. But looking back, rap battles were always very visual. If you ended a rap by saying your opponent was garbage, maybe you'd bust out a garbage bag and throw it at him. People use all kinds of things in battles to bring lyrics to life. Rap battling can be very physical—waving your arms to match your flow and shit, when you're all up in somebody's face. It's like being a conductor, only the orchestra you're conducting is your own stupid ass.

Paul and I were involved in choosing the beats for the battles. I was adamant about using the instrumental to Mobb Deep's "Shook Ones Pt. 2." That was *the* song in '95, so it worked perfectly for the period the movie was set in. The music was crucial. It helped maintain the authenticity of the whole thing. I was able to use the intensity I'd developed in battling but also demonstrate some of the control an actor needs to make the role believable. I think y'all believed me!

Proof and I used to go to St. Andrew's all the time to perform. It's one of the places where we got our start. The battle scenes in *8 Mile* were filmed on a set that was designed after the basement there, which is called The Shelter.

IT WAS THE STRAIGHT-UP DRAMATIC ACTING THAT WAS MORE OF A CHALLENGE.

Sometimes I'd say, "Curtis, I wouldn't say this," and he would say, "You're not you in this movie. You're Jimmy Smith, Jr." Yeah, okay, but the material was so parallel to my life that I felt like I really knew the stuff. We'd talk about the character and me in the third person: "I don't think Jimmy Smith, Jr. would say this. I don't think he would do this." And: "Marshall definitely wouldn't say this." I would ask Curtis if I could do a line the way I would say it, and he'd let me go for it. I don't think any of that stuff was used in the movie, though. I realized that we just had to trust each other, Curtis and I. He had to trust me on the music and the raps in the movie, and I had to trust him on the acting and directing. In that game, I was a student. And I was there to learn.

Some scenes were easier to shoot than others. The lovemaking scene probably took about a minute and a half to film. It wasn't fun—being basically naked in front of other men and women you don't know—but luckily I don't have too much of a problem showing my ass to the world. I'm the hip-hop Dirk Diggler. Then there were scenes that just took forever. The nighttime driving scenes were endless. The window would be down so the camera could get a close-up of my face, and I'd be driving in the wind in the winter in the dark: not cool.

The house-burning scene caused some drama in Detroit. Some folks protested. When I was coming up, there was this thing called Devil's Night, which used to go down the night before Halloween. Basically, kids would burn down abandoned houses, which were easy to come by in my hometown. The city of Detroit finally cracked down on it, but Devil's Night was definitely still poppin' during the time *8 Mile* is set, so it had to be a part of the flick. What we were trying to portray in the scene was something most of us can relate to: we all do stupid things as kids, and these kids are just fucking around. In the scene, I pick up a photograph—proof that a family once lived in this pit of a house. The scene shows how fucked up poverty can be, and points to the positive message of the movie: that no matter where you come from, whether it's the north side or the south side of 8 Mile, you can break out of it if your mentality and drive are right. Breaking out is the point of the film.

There was some weird shit in *8 Mile* too. I fought tooth and nail (and won) to get this scene with the horse out of the fucking movie because it made no sense whatsoever. Jimmy gets in a fight with his mother and takes his little sister next door to the babysitter, and then he sits down and starts crying, just thinking about his life and how fucked up everything is. But then he turns around and—get this—he sees a horse. As in one of those horses the cops ride through the city and shit. He sees this horse in a junkyard and he doesn't know why it's there. He walks up and starts petting it. Now, there's something about horses and the way they throw their heads up—they jerk their heads around out of fucking nowhere. Curtis kept telling me to grab the reins and pet it. But the horse was doing this crazy head-jerking movement, and I thought, Any minute this motherfucker's going to lift his head up and bust my fucking jaw and knock me the fuck out. Horses and me, we don't get on too well. I wouldn't fuck with a horse. If a horse dissed me, I wouldn't say anything back.

It was definitely a weird transition—the success, the explosion after *8 Mile*. Before the movie dropped, I wasn't defensive about my success. Sure, the white boy had sold millions, but I was good with it all. But I didn't know the buzz around the movie was going to get so big. You start to notice that parents are bringing their teenagers to your shows. I was thinking, What the fuck is going on? It got really fucking crazy after *8 Mile*. Interscope told me that the age range of my fan base went all the way up to people in their late 60s, early 70s—which completely didn't make sense to me. I mean, so you like me and your grandpa does too?

It's strange, you know, the new fans and where they come from. The core fans know what time it is, know about my history and my personal connections to the history of hip-hop. To everyone else—if you loved the movie, and from there you went on to love my music, and you're 86 years old—I just want to say thank you. Hailie thanks you. Her college is paid for.

AS AN UNDERGROUND ARTIST STARTING OUT, I NEVER WANTED TO SELL OUT,

but I'm sure there are fans who think I have. To them I say, I still love you. I don't feel like I made music that sold me out. I made pop joints, yes, but my lyrics and flow and command of the beat were always pure hip-hop all the way. I was spitting the same. The only difference was that a whole lot more people were checking me out and supporting my art. I hope you all understand that I can't control who likes my music or who likes me.

Seriously though, if I do another movie, the challenge is going to be whether I can take on a role that has nothing to do with the real me. When you think of a really good actor, like Denzel Washington, who's probably my favorite actor of all time, you know Denzel is serious. Whether he slips into the role of a gangster or a cop, you forget you're watching a movie. The challenge for me is to be able to present the kind of range that a serious cat like Denzel has. He's an inspiration. If I'm going to do something I need to be the best at it. I need to be super-competitive. Respected.

6 ANGER MANAGEMENT

I'VE ALWAYS HAD ISSUES WITH MY TEMPER.

When I look back at myself during those years when everything was blowing up, I think maybe at first I was a little, you know, too aggressive and loud. It was like I had this voice and I had to be heard. "Don't fuck with me," to the point where people must have been wondering, Why is this dude so angry? Is he on crack? Is he on fucking crystal meth? I go back and see old interviews and even now I wonder, Why was I so hyper?

I went through a phase back then when I was fucking shooting pistols in the air behind the studio and, you know, pulling guns out on motherfuckers, pointing a pistol in somebody's face, not even realizing that I could've gone to jail for that shit.

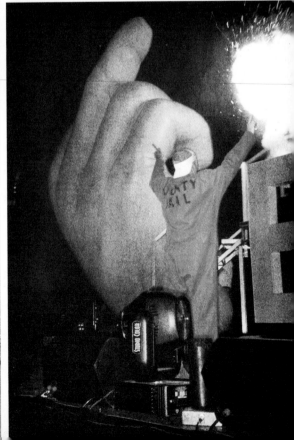

Back then I was living on a main road, Hayes Street, and random people used to come and knock on my door all the time. The first album had gone four times platinum. I finally had some money. I remember thinking, I have a house, I can park in back. It was the first time in my life I'd had a real home that I could call my own and nobody was going to be able to throw me out. Directly across the street there was a fucking trailer park. Wouldn't you know it? Sometimes kids would sit and wait for me to come out.

Other times they didn't even bother to wait. They would just come and bang on the door. The doorbell kept ringing. I was starting to lose it. As soon as I would open the front door the camera flashes would go off. They'd start *clapping*. I was losing my mind. I got up in one kid's face with a pistol. Unloaded, but still. Was that the right thing to do? Hell, no. But my temper was out of control. Thank God I was in enough control to not do something tragic. I had to move out of there before I wound up hurting somebody.

The very first pistol I ever owned, I bought legally. I mean, I didn't have the CCW, but the gun was licensed.

THIS LITTLE PIECE OF STEEL WOULD GET ME
IN A GANG OF TROUBLE,

like the parking lot incident that went down. You've heard the deal—it was me, the gun, some dude with Kim, and a parking lot with cars and people in it,

ROYAL OAK
POLICE DEPARTMENT

LAST:	MATHERS
FIRST:	MARSHALL
DOB:	10 / 17 / 72
SEX:	MALE
RACE:	WHITE
HEIGHT:	508
WEIGHT:	155
EYES:	HAZEL
HAIR:	BLOND OR STR
EVENT#:	2401906

IMAGE CAPTURED: /   /

Above: My beef with the Insane Clown Posse goes way back, but after the 2000 incident in Royal Oak, somebody called the police. I know I can't compare the couple of weekends I spent in jail to the time some other people have had to do—10, 20, 30 years, life. I'm lucky that all I really had to deal with was court (right) and probation, but it still sucked.

Hey, y'all have to recognize that I'm a man with a plan. True, they're not always the best-laid-out plans, but there's some thought that goes into my moves. So I saw an episode of *Cops* that was based in Michigan, right? The episode said that in the state of Michigan you can get a mandatory year for each bullet if you don't have a concealed weapon license. My idiotic logic at the time was to never have more than three bullets in my gun. That way, if I got caught I figured I would only do three years. Eventually I did go and apply for that CCW. When the board asked me why I needed a gun, I said, "Well, I've already sold three million records . . ." Finally they

approved me. All I had to do was take a safety course, which I started but never completed. Anyway, that's why I blame it all on *Cops*.

So I went down to that parking lot with a gun and no bullets. *Guns are bad*, I tell you. The whole thing ended with me being accused of pistol-whipping a man who was kissing my wife. The thing was, that same weekend, I had a little scuffle with this guy who was working for some old enemies, the Detroit-based Insane Clown Posse (ICP). That shit was not helping my cause, especially since there was a gun involved there too. I caught three felony charges in one weekend. And I was completely sober. No pills. Just passion. Millions of people can relate to that crime-of-passion shit.

It's not like I didn't have run-ins with the law before. The first time I got in trouble, it was just Proof and me and this other guy messing around. Sometimes we'd go out and bust our guns—*paintball* guns—at some random Detroit folk. We'd do it every Friday night, after putting it on at Saint Andrew's Hall. This was around '92—a great time for hip-hop, by the way—before I got a record deal. I was 20. This one night we were basically driving around shooting paintballs from the car. I turned down the wrong street and we ended up near Wayne State University, where we ran into these white kids on skateboards. Proof snuck up behind one of them and shot him in the back of the head, like three times—POW! POW! POW!—with the paint pellets. Now, at close range, those motherfuckers hurt! You know what I'm saying? But this kid acted like he was on acid or something. I mean, he didn't move, he didn't cover his head, he just kept *skating*. It was like some *Twilight Zone* shit. Next thing you know, there's fucking sirens, and five cop cars pull up.

One particular cop kicked the shit out of us. He had me facedown on somebody's lawn, with cuffs on. Another one of the cops grabbed my earring and was like, "You like to wear earrings, huh, you little faggot? You little white boy?" I had these small hoops on, and he just ripped them out. He made Proof eat grass, literally took grass and shoved it in his mouth. At some point this lady cop said something like, "Uh, people have video cameras now." This was all happening right around Rodney King. Man, I wish somebody had taped it.

Proof and I got in the same squad car—got thrown in, that is. We were both cuffed. And I said to him, "Damn, they fucked you up." He was like, "They fucked *me* up? Look at you!" They didn't want to have us take mug shots because of how bad we looked. Afterward, I had bruised ribs. My mother was real lawsuit happy, so she took pictures of my ribs. They hurt like hell.

We wound up going to two Detroit jails, and while we were in one of those roach-infested holding pens we

...HOLY SHIT, THERE GO OUR RAP CAREERS.

found out that one of us had shot somebody in . . . the dick. We hit somebody in the balls with balls: paintballs! The guy wanted to press charges, and the cops were telling us it was a felonious assault—that we were looking at *five years*, at least. We sat down with this detective, and he's like, "Can you afford an attorney?" We were fucked. It was like, Holy shit, there go our rap careers. There goes everything.

But then it turned out that no one we'd shot showed up in court, so we got off on a technicality. When we left the courthouse I remember feeling like, Whew! Oh my God, thank you, Jesus!

So, yeah, I've dealt with my fair share of cops and courtrooms, but the incidents with the *real* gun were the most notorious. I got probation for the ICP thing. For the alleged pistol-whipping, I pleaded guilty to carrying a concealed weapon and the judge let me off on the assault charge. The catch was that I had to go for anger management counseling. It isn't a stretch to imagine how the name for my infamous Anger Management Tours came out of me having to take those classes. They were supposed to get me back on track and keep me out of jail. The whole thing wasn't that intense. I showed up, talked to a dude, and went home. I don't want to say it didn't help, but it wasn't anything too deep.

MY MOOD CAN CHANGE QUICKLY.

It's always been that way. When I was drinking, I could be in a good mood—just loving everybody and feeling like everything was great—then somebody would say the wrong shit to me, and before you knew it there was nothing my bodyguards could do to stop me from reacting and at least punching, spitting, or kicking a few times before they could get to me. It would be the simplest shit that would set me off, like somebody looking at me hard. And I could not stop until I felt like I'd done something to make that person accountable, to make that person learn his lesson. Afterward, I would be full of apologies, just saying "I'm sorry" over and over. I'd feel like such an idiot for acting like that. Like, Why can't I control this?

You all saw the Triumph thing go down at the MTV Video Music Awards, right? That's a pretty perfect example. I mean, there I am, sitting in my seat, and they announce that I'm up for an award, presented by Christina Aguilera. I had said some things about her in the past, Moby had said some things about me, and I had said some things back about him. So I'm sitting there next to Proof, and they bring in Moby and sit him like two rows directly behind us. So now I'm like, Okay, what's going on? What are they trying to do? I've got Moby behind me, and Christina up onstage, and then this dog puppet gets up in my face. I'd been so busy touring and doing my own shit that I hadn't had time to watch TV, so I had no idea what that dog was. All I saw was Moby and Christina and this dude who's sticking his hand in my face, trying to be funny. I didn't even see the puppet, you know? My natural reaction was, "Get the fuck out of my face. Get your fucking hand out of my face." And that's when I kind of

lost it and a half. I should have kept my composure, but instead I stuck my fingers basically on Moby's nose. Right in his face, like, "Fuck you."

When they told me I won the award, I went up there and gave Christina a hug, because there wasn't a real beef with her. I was just dissing her to separate myself 'cause I didn't want to be classified as a pop artist. When I hugged her, I thought I was being as mature as I could be. But when I got behind closed doors in the green room, I threw a fucking fit. There was a cooler with drinks in it, and I asked if anybody wanted to grab a water or something. Nobody did. So I picked up the cooler and threw it against the wall and kind of fucked up the whole room, basically.

The thing is, in the hip-hop world, when you talk about someone, you might not want to see them, because you don't know what's going to happen. With Moby, it wasn't like I literally wanted to physically put hands on him. It's just that all my life I'd been trained to react a certain way when put in a situation like that. My instinct was, someone talks about you, you see them, you fight. But *Moby*? Really? I was going to fight *Moby*? I was going to fight a *puppet*? I don't know if anybody will even understand it now. It was basically just too many different things at once—Moby, Christina, the puppet . . . I was like, Okay, someone's *really* fucking with me.

In hindsight, I should have handled it differently, and I truly believe that if I were in that situation again, knowing the whole shtick with the puppet dog, I *would* have acted differently. What I actually got mad about was the most ridiculous thing in the fucking world. A puppet.

This is the kind of shit that happens that makes me think to myself, Maybe you need to go back to anger management class. Because, obviously, I haven't learned. Even now, part of me feels like, Eminem, whenever you drink you get violent. Another part of me is like, No, whenever somebody fucks with me, I get violent. And if I'm drunk and someone fucks with me, it's even worse. This is one reason why I never go out.

This problem is not something I'm proud of. I mean, I'm a lot better than I used to be. I am. But it's still messed up. I'm 35 years old. I'm a dad now. Once you hit 30, you're supposed to at least be a half-grown-ass man, you know what I mean? The truth is, a lot of things put me on edge. Even today. It can be something as simple as being asked a million stupid questions, or a rapper who's not on my level trying to come up by starting beef with me. So many things. God knows, 10 years down the road I don't want my daughters hearing about all this somewhere and going, "He thinks it's cool to act like this." Because I don't. The moral of this story is not that it's alright to

walk around with my fucking chest stuck out saying, "Look at me. I'm Mister Fucking Tough Guy."

But, you know, when you grow up like I did—bouncing around, fighting for everything—it does make you angry. It just does. It's something I've kind of tried to block out, but when I do think back about how many schools I went to and everything else, it makes me realize, No wonder I was so mad at everything. It was almost a way for me piss back in the face of the people who pissed on me all my life, to get back at every bully who

ever picked on me, every person who ever fucked with me growing up. The fact that Hailie's life is so different than mine is one of my proudest achievements.

I do think age has made a difference. Hailie and Alaina are getting older, and I'm not taking so many things to heart like I used to. I mean, I still have a temper, but I have more control now. The stakes are high, and my family comes first. Marshall Mathers behind bars isn't cute, and Eminem behind bars is terrible for business.

TODD K. NELSON

1961 – 2004

Guns and violence have been around me my whole life—in my family life, in my social life, everywhere. I've just always had a fascination with them. I'm not saying I was a thug or that I dealt drugs or murdered people. That's just how I was raised—step up or get stepped on—so I never really thought it was a problem, you know?

When I was 11, living in Missouri, my uncles would take me to the gun range to bust guns. AK-47s. They'd let me empty off the whole clip. When I was seven years old I was handling my uncle Todd's Colt .45—the same Colt he allegedly ended up murdering a dude with in a supermarket parking lot. He had me shooting at beer cans at that age. Sounds crazy, but it's true. Anybody who has a

gun will tell you that at first it makes them feel powerful. I was infatuated. Obviously I don't feel that way now. I've lost too many friends, family members, loved ones to gun violence. I would much rather use my fists. (Kidding.)

I wasn't super tight with my uncle Todd, but he was my uncle just the same. He was troubled, but he wasn't a bad guy. To a certain extent, he was there for me—kind of like a much older brother I didn't know that well. Sure, he wasn't a perfect man, but he loved kids. He was convicted for killing a guy who was supposedly a child molester, and served his time. When he got out a few years back, he killed himself—blew his brains out on my birthday. It was very confusing for me. Really,

he was a well-intentioned dude who just couldn't function in society.

Depression must run in my family. My other uncle, Ronnie, committed suicide when I was 19 years old, and it was one of the most difficult times in my life. I got the phone call at Kim's house, and it didn't register at first. I threw the phone down and just dropped to my knees. I didn't go to the funeral—it was back in Missouri—because I wanted to remember him the way I remembered him. I didn't want to see him in a box. I guess I was able to go to Proof's funeral because I'd become a man by then. And with all due respect, Ronnie's head was *gone*—and it was an open casket. I didn't understand that. The man blew his head off with a shotgun—why the hell would you have an open-casket viewing?

When Ronnie was seven years old, he burned my grandmother's house down. When he was 11, he put a hamster in the microwave—it exploded. He was just always doing this crazy shit. He was also taking a lot of whippings from one of my grandmother's husbands. When my grandmother was married to that guy (he's an ex-husband now), I saw the whippings and even saw Ronnie getting thrown down the stairs. I think all that abuse twisted him up. A lot of people in my family had screws loose because of abuse. If you go back and look at the abuse that I took, it's no surprise I became who I am. Someone I don't really want to be.

7 FAMILY MAN

BEING A DAD MAKES ME FEEL POWERFUL

in a way that I hadn't known before, and it's the kind of power I don't want to abuse. It's the kind of power that helps me overcome the bad shit from my childhood. It's like I'm rewriting my own history.

In my life I have a daughter, Hailie, a niece, Alaina, and another little girl, Whitney, who isn't biologically mine. All three of my girls call me Daddy. They're all loved the same and they all get the same treatment. Because of my success, I've been able to provide for them in ways my family never could for me. That's what it's all

Who looks this good at four years old?

about. Rapping is how I took control of my life, and now of my girls' lives. I can only imagine how the things I've been able to offer them would have helped a young me.

I try to explain to the girls how lucky we are to have simple things like car rides to and from school, but I think it's going to be some time before they understand where I came from and what Dad truly did for them. I've seen both sides of the tracks, the suburbs and the city. Whether it was a white or black or mixed community that I lived in, I was always poor. Always. Welfare cheese, Farina, powdered milk—the whole nine yards. I was lucky if I got my two little outfits from Kmart a year.

I want my girls to have a place where they belong and feel protected. That's why I say my biggest accomplishment is being a father and why I stepped back from the rap game for a minute. You can't just show up once in a while and call yourself Dad. Back when I was touring all

the time, the summer tours were my favorite because I could bring the girls with me a lot. I'd bring Kim on the road too, and it just worked. Other times, if I had to be away from them for a while, it would get to the point where I would miss them so much that I'd come back. I'd have one day off, and I'd be flying on a private plane home, seeing them for the day, flying back the next day, and catching up with the tour at the last minute.

I haven't toured since 2005, but I still bust my ass. I told one of my daughters, "Dad works so hard because I don't want you to live like I had to live." You try to explain these things to a 12-year-old or a 15-year-old, and they'll answer back, "Well, why *should* we live like that?" I won't front, it kind of hurts to hear that. But they don't understand. It's just a phase they're going through.

I want them to go to college. I try to instill educational values in them. But it can be tough when you didn't graduate high school and your education level is 8th grade. I failed 9th grade three times, and I'm trying to argue with them about going to college?! I try to explain that Dad made a bad decision to quit school. I just got lucky. I really did hit the lottery. I know that talent plays into it, but there are a lot of people out there with talent. If it weren't for Dre giving me that chance and if I hadn't had people like Proof in my life who pushed me, we'd be in a trailer somewhere.

Top left: I'm not sure who got to say I was an Indian and not a Pilgrim. I'd like to say that being onstage was natural in kindergarten, but I don't really remember this day! Who knows what school I was in? It looks like it was pretty mixed, though.

Right: There are times when I look at Hailie and think that she looks just like me. She doesn't have my ears, though. Thank God. When I was a kid, my ears were stupid big. I had to deal with nicknames like "Mickey." As in Mouse.

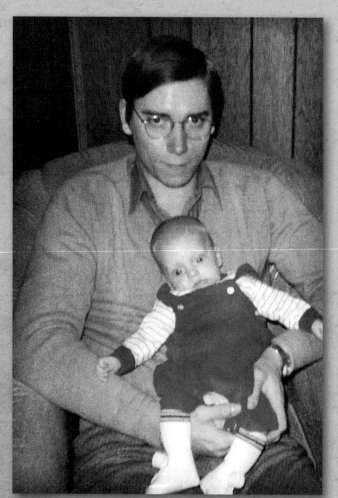

4/14/90 - Easter Eve

THE WORST PART
ABOUT THE WAY I GREW UP WAS THAT
I NEVER HAD A REAL HOME.

I was always bouncing around from school to school, and the moving hurt my interest in education. I went to two different kindergartens in Missouri. One was in a trailer park, where each class had a trailer. I'll never forget: my great-aunt Edna would walk me to school when I was five years old and she was like 60. Anybody who's listened to my music already knows the sob story of my childhood. In "Evil Deeds" I talk about how I was taken from doorstep to doorstep: "Father, please forgive me for I know not what I do, I just never got the chance to ever meet you." Obviously, that's an exaggeration. The lyrics are a metaphor for how I felt. Then I say, "Till somebody finally took me in, my great-aunt and uncle, Edna and Charles." That part is dead true. Charles was my father's uncle, who fought in World War II, and Edna was his wife. They were my saving grace. Starting when my parents divorced, I stayed with them a lot.

Their home was a safe haven for me, a place where I could just sit on the floor in front of the TV and color and stuff like that. Uncle Charles died about 15 years ago, and Edna lives alone. She's 94 now. She's proud, man, she just won't accept anything from me when it comes to money, and I want to help her so bad, you know? If I try to send money, she sends it back with a card, saying, "Brucie, I'm going to kick your ass." I speak to her on a regular basis. She doesn't want anything except conver-

sation. It's one of the reasons I love her so much. Her love is genuine.

I'm not going to lie: I'm always going to have questions about my dad. But at this point, I've decided that I'll never have them answered—so fuck it. Fuck him. I'm beyond wanting to know the dude. It takes a real special kind of asshole to abandon a kid. To keep in touch with other family members—like his uncle—but not even get on the phone with a kid who did nothing wrong. There's just no excuse as a parent to do what he did. I don't care if they were lost in Alaska or the fucking desert somewhere, I would find my little girls.

Top left: This is the only picture of my father that my mother ever had when I was a kid. She showed it to me when we were living on Dresden on the East Side.

Top right: I remember those pants real well. They were loose, MC Hammer–style pants. I had this red pair and I had a green pair. I wore them to school practically every day, with some black kicks. And yes, that is a high-top fade! Back then, all I thought about was Kid 'n Play.

Bottom left: Nice outfit! No one can tell me exactly where this was taken, but something about the way I'm sitting alone on the steps makes me think that it was just before or just after moving to yet another house.

Bottom right: I was five or six months old in this picture. Supposedly that was right around when my parents split up, and I was dropped off with Aunt Edna and Uncle Charles.

I TRIED TO HAVE A NORMAL
IN SPITE OF EVERYTHING, BUT

LIFE AS A KID IT WAS ROUGH.

I tried to be social. To fit in. I really did. But, like I said, every time, just as I would start to get comfortable and make friends—BOOM! We'd be moving again. When you've just transferred to a new school, you know how that shit is—it sucks. You don't know anybody, so you've got to start over and re-get to know everybody. Recently I was trying to remember all the schools I went to. I had a very long list, and I don't even think it was complete. It started to make me sad. I used to think that to fail in school as many times as I did was my fault. But in hindsight, was it?

Making new friends every couple of months ain't easy for any kid, but it was especially hard for me because I was so quiet. Shy. I was getting beaten up, and I would get nosebleeds and then sometimes my ear would bleed. That was Marshall Mathers. Never was social. Never had too many friends. Which goes against the image I put out there with my music, as an emcee who's up in your face with all kinds of opinions and shit to talk. That's Eminem. Truth is, I've never felt like I belonged.

We moved to Warren, just outside Detroit, when I was about to turn 14. We were staying with my grandmother on Timken Street because we didn't have a place to live and she wouldn't make us pay rent. That's how I ended up going to Lincoln, in the suburbs. I went to some of 7th grade and all of 8th grade there. That was the longest I ever went to one school. I started meeting a lot of Chaldean kids, and they became my first real friends. There were a few black kids in there, but it was mostly whites and Chaldeans, who are Christian Iraqis that settled in Detroit. (Here's something crazy about Detroit: Saddam Hussein got the key to the city in 1980. He gave a bunch of money to a Chaldean church and he got the key to the city.)

By the time I was supposed to start 9th grade, we had moved to the East Side of Detroit. So I wasn't able to carry my friends into high school, and high school is the biggest transition in your life. I put a lot of blame on myself because I could have enrolled in Osborn instead, but I didn't. When you grow up like that, with the moving and never fitting in and getting bullied, it makes you angry. It just does. Especially when you go back and think about it. So it's something I've tried to block out.

Sometimes my mom gave me money to buy cigarettes for her. She'd give me four bucks for two packs of Winston Light 100s, and I'd steal the cigarettes and keep the money to buy my lunch. I was on the free lunch list at school because we were always on welfare, which is embarrassing. Most of my friends were in the free lunch program, and they will tell you exactly how degrading it was. The worst was if there was a hot chick standing behind you, or one of the football players. I used to be terrified of those dudes because they were bigger than me, and they all hung in packs. So you'd get to the front of the line and you'd have to say, "I'm on the free lunch list," to some old lady who could barely see. She's got her

glasses all crooked and shit. You'd be like, "My name is Mathers." And the old lady, who could also barely hear, would shout, "OH, YOU SAID YOU'RE ON THE FREE LUNCH LIST, HONEY?" And she'd check again and be like, "I DON'T . . . I DON'T SEE YOU HERE. WHAT'S YOUR NAME AGAIN? MATHERS?" This was the deal at every school I ever went to. So the rare times when I could buy my lunch, I felt proud.

Man, when I was 17, times were rough: I wasn't living at home at that time for a variety of reasons, so sometimes I'd catch a stay over at Proof's mother's house and sleep on the couch. Other times, I'd catch a stay at Kim's mother's house. Basically, it was a situation where I had to get in where I fit in. But I always figured out some-

It was like that when Hailie was born too. Kim and were always trying to figure out how to get from one day to the next. We were so young, and we struggled like crazy. I was working at this factory, where I swept the floor and cleaned the machinery with that mineral spirits stuff that's no damn good—crazy toxic. I was doing everything from sandblasting, to sweeping floors, to doing dishes in the little kitchen area—anything I could do to make money. Anything.

I was flippin' burgers and moppin' and cleanin' like you'd never believe. I was like Mayor McCheese with robot arms that were perfect for just moppin' and moppin' and moppin'. Holding Hailie was easy because my arms were so strong from flippin' burgers and moppin Kim's family helped us out, which was a beautiful thing Mostly, though, Kim and I grinded. Hard.

We couldn't afford to live anywhere nice, and we could barely afford to live in the shit houses we were living in, so we were always getting evicted. I was trying to rap, go to The Hip Hop Shop, and do all those things—we couldn't even afford gas to go to work.

We were getting robbed, too, but we started getting hip to that game Whoever would rob the house would wrap all the stuff up in a blanket, go throw it in the alley somewhere, and pick it up later. So we'd go to the alley to get all our shit back. We went to a pawn shop once and found our TV. We'd taken a black marker and made a little tiny mark on it, and that's how we knew it was our TV. When you get robbed in the same house five times—and the guy is so comfortable robbing your house that he takes his jacket off and leaves it on your couch, and he makes himself a peanut butter and jelly sandwich—you figure some things out. I'd be sleeping on the floor with Hailie and Kim, just waiting for this guy to show up.

We came home this one time and heard what sounded like an army of people running down the stairs, so we ran outside. Hailie was still strapped into her car seat and I sat down on the lawn because I didn't know what to do. This guy came out the side door, and it looked like he just had a screwdriver in his hand, so I chased after

butcher knife, so I went back into the house. The only thing I could find was a frying pan, so I grabbed it. I chased him up the block, he jumped this fence, and he was gone. That's when I went from having a frying pan underneath the couch to having a little .25-caliber pistol under there. I never caught that dude.

One time Kim was so scared that she took the baby to her mom's. I was down in Atlanta with Bizarre, and Kim called and said the guy had robbed the house for the fourth time and that I needed to come home immediately. She was terrified to stay there by herself, and I guess I don't blame her.

There came a point around then when I had just sort of given up. Times were so hard. Christmas was the worst. I talk about that in "Mockingbird": "Mommy wrapped the Christmas presents up and stuck them under the tree, / And said some of them were from me / 'Cause Daddy couldn't buy them." I'll never forget that

This is the place on Fairport where we started D12. We had a beat box and a drum machine in the basement and we would take turns recording our rhymes on Denaun's four-track. We also got robbed five times here.

♡ HAILIE ⚡ ALAINA ♡

DADDY
↓

"MY"   "BAND"

LOVES YOU!!

Christmas. I sat up the whole night crying. When I listen to that song, to this day I still shed a tear. Or two. Or three. Every word in that song is true.

It was one of those situations where it was like, I have this little girl, and, you know, that's my world. And that's when I just knew I had to kick it in gear. Christmas for us is a lot different these days. Thank you, Jesus. Allah. Buddha. God. Thank you sincerely.

Above: My "other" band is the kind that doesn't sell records.

Opposite top: Me and Kim, happy and a long time ago.

Opposite bottom left: This wasn't very long after Hailie was born. If you look closely, you can see my hair is still dark and I'm wearing a T-shirt from The Hip Hop Shop.

Opposite bottom right: In 1999 I flew Hailie and Kim to Los Angeles while I was recording *The Marshall Mathers LP* with Dre. I used to make that sad face—we called it the boo-boo face—because as soon as I did, Hailie'd come running over to hug me. It's part of that special relationship you have with your kids when they're young. Like, instantly she'd become Daddy's little girl.

My girls' lives are pretty stable. They live in one house (well, two when you count Kim's), they go to one school, and they have the love and support of two parents. Kim and I have had our differences, sure, but things are good between us now. I'm not away from home as much as I used to be, but when I do have to step away she's there holding the fort down—and she does an amazing job. It's great that we've been able to come to an understanding. That's a big source of stress that I'm glad is behind my ass.

I try to teach my girls to be responsible and accountable. Their world isn't just a free-for-all. They've got things they have to do around the house. When they get older, they'll have to get jobs and learn about what it means to earn. The safety net will of course be there—I'll always support them—but I want to support them going out and doing things for themselves too. Going for it. They're good kids, and I'm not just saying that because they're mine. Kids will be kids and, yeah, mine misbehave and get punished once in a while. They keep me grounded. For real. And they make me laugh so hard. Eminem: concerned and involved parent. Not what you would expect, huh?

I'm protective of them, and I try my best to guard them from the ugly stuff that I have done or said. Whitney's too young to understand my "Rot in Pieces" tattoo, so I'm never shirtless around the house. One time, the girls had a bunch of friends over, and the 10 o'clock news had an item about Eminem assaulting some dude. I'm trying to change the channel so the kids don't hear it, but one of them does and runs and gets the rest. They're all crowding around the TV, and I'm trying to defuse it by saying, "What Dad did was bad. This is not Dad!"

Sometimes I worry about what they'll think about my lyrics when they're all grown up. I can't protect them forever. People have said that my songs have really hateful lyrics about women. Most of the early anger stemmed from my relationship with Kim. We'd get into arguments and break up, and then I'd write a song that was sort of like, "Fuck bitches, I hate them all." And the way I would explain it to Kim was that this is how I was feeling at the moment. So she wouldn't really put up a fight about putting the songs out. The songs were basically describing our relationship, but I was always mixing in a little bit of something else I'd experienced with someone else. Kim understood, but I wasn't thinking, Fuck, my kids are going to get older, and they're going to hear this. I

Hailie 6 months

realized pretty quickly that you get to the point where the kids ain't stupid. When that day comes for my girls, I'll tell them that when Daddy would get mad at Mom, Daddy would make a song, and that's how I vented.

That day is probably going to come soon. Shit, maybe it's already here. Hailie's going into the 7th grade now. When she wants to do something and she applies herself, she just gets it done. It's weird to see that in her because it reminds me so much of me. I would never wish fame on any of them. We have this ongoing joke in the house: I'll tell Hailie, "Well, if you want to dance, you can dance. But when you get to a certain age, you're going to stop, because you are not going to be famous."

Dad

When you came home tonight
Our circle was complete
I felt secure as you tucked me in
And kissed me on the cheek
A story, a prayer then lights out
Then you and Mom closed the door
And I'd try to hear your whispers
Till my eyes wouldn't open anymore
I Thank God for blessing me
With His goodness from above
By making you my Dad
For you filled my
Life
With love

I try to protect their privacy as much as I can, and, believe me, it's hard. Hailie's name is out there the most, but could you point her out in a lineup? No. She's almost this character in my raps. When you're famous, it's like every little thing you do is public. When I do try to do regular things with the kids, it can get to be a circus. Right now, with fucking camera phones and shit like that, I am so paranoid. Take as many fucking pictures as you want of me, just don't snap the kids. I want them to be able to do regular things and function as normally as possible.

LADIES AND GENTLEMEN, RAISING KIDS AIN'T EASY.

DON'T TRY IT AT HOME WITHOUT PARENTAL SUPERVISION.

Seriously, it's a challenge raising them. I am a single parent who is partners with another single parent—Kim. We're a good team now, though, and the back and forth between our households is seamless. It's become a normal reality for the kids. My dad role is more important than my *8 Mile* role or my emcee role. But I'll never forget about the mic and the rhymes and talking my shit. Hailie's daddy is still a better rapper than your daddy.

When my girls do sweet things for me, I remember that I'm a lucky man.

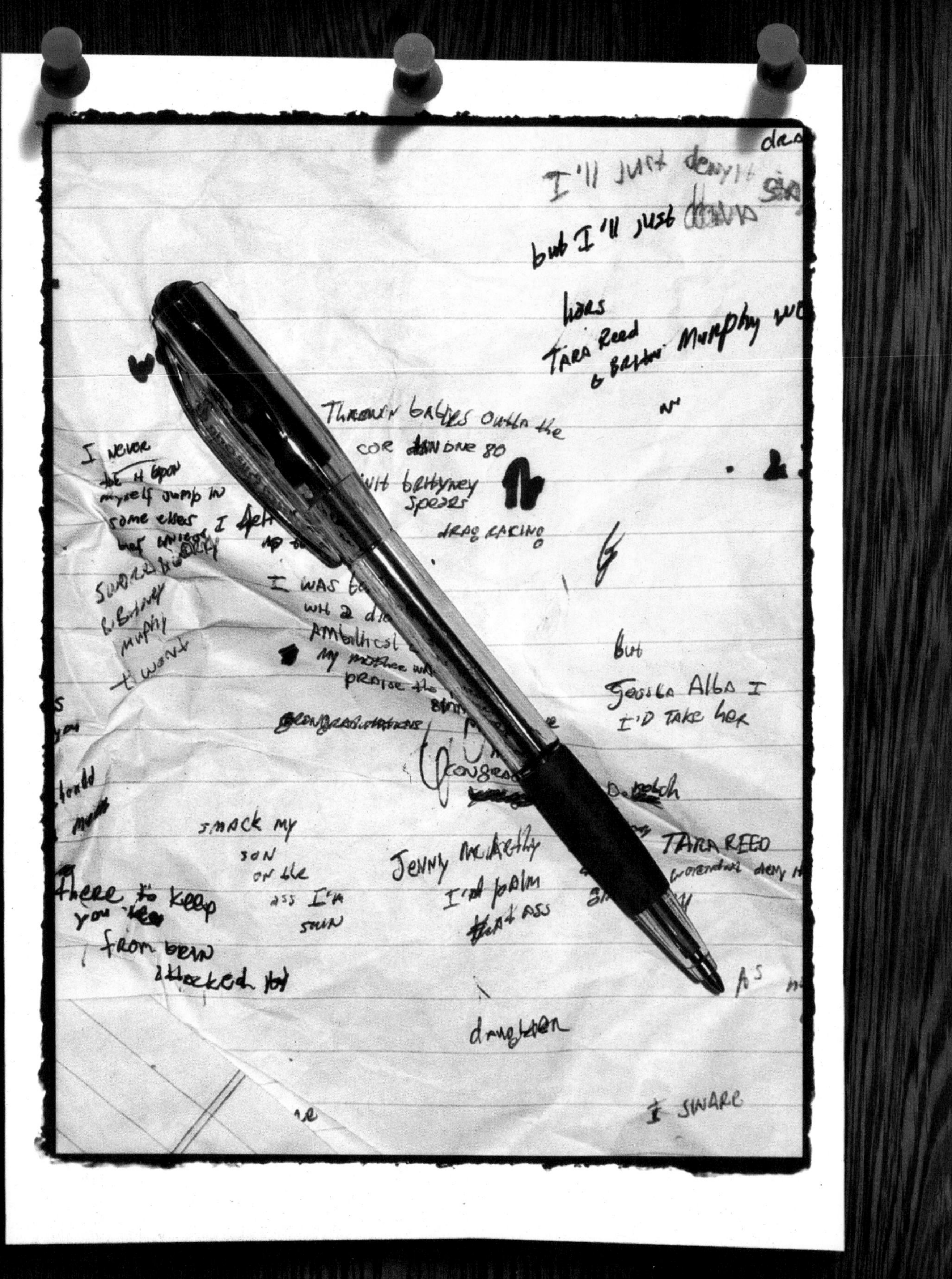

GHOST TRAPPED IN A BEAT:

ORIGINAL HANDWRITTEN LYRICS FROM THE PERSONAL COLLECTION
OF MARSHALL B. MATHERS III

I USED TO KEEP MY LYRIC SHEETS CRUMPLED UP IN A BAG.

I figured it was easy to carry a bag around, but the bag got bigger and bigger. That was the crazy part about it—it got so heavy even though it was only full of paper. People would ask, "What the fuck you got in here, man? You got rocks in here?" I'd say, "No." They'd open it up, and there would be all this paper. It was years' worth of lyrics—maybe two or three years—and that's a lot for me. I still have the bag. I dumped it out and that's how I found a lot of this stuff.

Reading my lyric sheets even gets confusing for me sometimes. I have a hard time understanding what's going on. But when I'm actually working on the songs, I know exactly where everything is and what it's sup-

posed to mean. When I go back years later, I have to ask myself, How the fuck did I go from here to there? I'll skip words so people can't ever figure out where I'm going, just in case my written words slip away into the wrong hands. This is for my own personal lyrical protection.

When it comes to writing, though, things just come to me. I can be anywhere. If I get an idea real quick, I'll jot it down on whatever. I don't care where it goes. I've just got to get it down on paper, right then and there, or I'll lose it. Eventually they all end up in a rap somewhere. Dr. Dre always says, "Man, look at this little chicken scratch shit! I could never understand this, even if I wanted to."

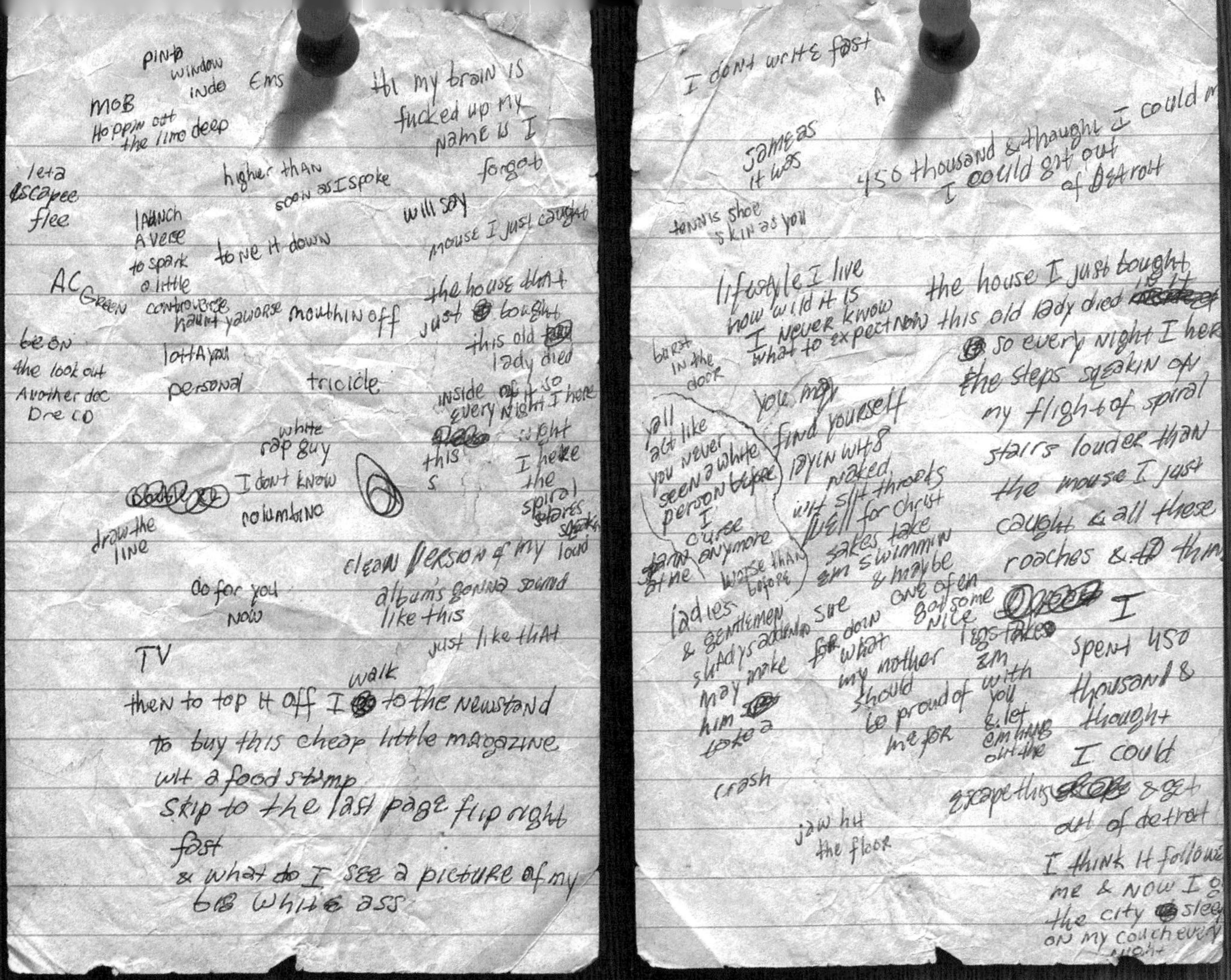

Handwritten notes (left page):

MOB
PINK
window
inde Ems
Hoppin out
the limo deep

tbl my brain is
fucked up my
name is I

let a
escapee
flee

higher than
soon as I spoke

forgot

I launch
A vere
to spark
a little

to ne it down

will say

mouse I just caught

AC
GREEN controversy
haunt ya worse mouthin off

the house didn't
just @ bought

be on
the look out
Another doc
Dre CD

lotta you

personal   tricicle

this old
lady died

inside of it so
every night I here

white
rap guy
I don't know
columbine

draw the
line

this
s

I here
the
spiral
stairs
speak

do for you
now

clean version of my loud
albums gonna sound
like this

just like that

TV

walk
then to top it off I @ to the newsstand
to buy this cheap little magazine
wit a food stamp
skip to the last page flip right
fast
& what do I see a picture of my
6B white ass

Handwritten notes (right page):

I don't write fast

A

same as
it was

450 thousand & thought I could m
I could get out
of Detroit

tennis shoe
skin as you

lifestyle I live
how wild it is
I never know
what to expect now

the house I just bought
this old lady died
so every night I her
the steps squeakin on
my flight of spiral
stairs louder than
the mouse I just
caught & all these
roaches & th

burst
in the
door

y'all
act like
you never
seen a white
person before
I
curse
anymore

you may
find yourself
layin wit8
naked
wit slit throats
well for christ
sakes take
em swimmin
worse than & maybe
before

ladies
& gentlemen
s lady's askin sure
may make for doin what
him take a should
be proud of
me for

one often
boy some
nice legs take

my mother

I
spent 450
thousand &
thought
I could
& get
out of detroit

crash

jaw hit
the floor

escape this & get

em hand
out the
with
you
& let

I think it follow
me & now I
the city sleg
on my couch eve
night

This page dates back to when I started recording with Dr. Dre in 1998, but there's an idea that ended up in "Rain Man" on *Encore* years later: "My name is I forgot." That one line took a while to get spit back out. And you might recognize a few

I think I wrote "I spent 450 thousand..." after I bought my first house. I had finally gotten out of the city and moved to the suburbs, to that nice house in Sterling Heights, right across from the trailer park. I was fucking nuts in that house, wilding out. I was doing things I wasn't really supposed to. I guess you can take the white rapper out of the trailer park, but you can't take the—

I used to circle lyrics that I thought I might use. Or write them in a different-colored ink. "Y'all act like you never seen a white person before." I went back and dug that line out for "The Real

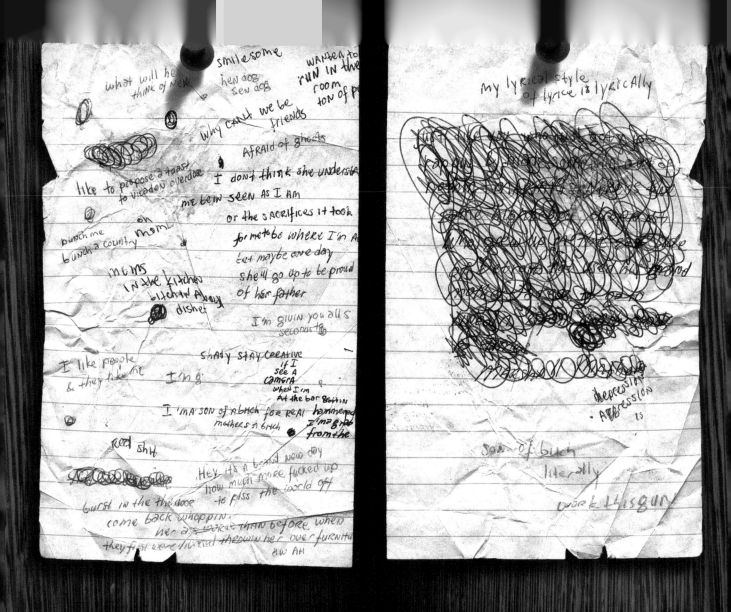

what will he smilesome
think of Next hen dog
sew dog

WANTED to
RUN IN the
room
ton of p

Why CANT we be friends

AFRAID of ghosts

like to propose a toast
to vicoden overdose

I don't think she understa
me bein seen AS I AM
or the sacrifices it took
for me to be where I'm A

bunch me oh mom
bunch a country

moms
in the kitchen
bitchin Abouy
dishes

but maybe one day
she'll go up to be proud
of her father

I'm givin you all 5
seconds to

I like people
& they like me

SHADy STAY CREATIVE
I'm if I
see A
camera
when I'm
At the bar sittin

I'm A SON of A bitch for REAL hammered
mothers a bitch I'm a gro
from the

Real shit

Hey its a brand new day
how much more fucked up
to piss the world off

burst in the the door
come back whoppin
her a worse than before when
they first were divine threw her over furnitu
AW AH

my lyrical style
of lyrics is lyrically

depression
· Aggression is

son of bitch
literally

over this gun

The lines at the bottom of this sheet ended up in the beginning of "The Real Slim Shady." I have no idea how I kicked out that song. I had the hook in my head, and I just needed lyrics. I was so tapped out, scrambling for a song, and lines from different

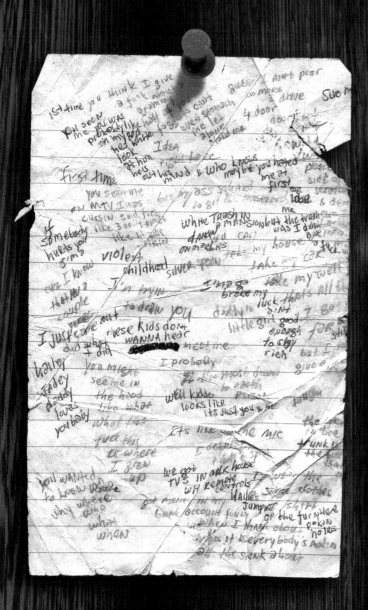

Those lines up at the top left made it into "The Real Slim Shady." Instead of "critics," though, it looks like I originally wrote "faggots." Now, I've already talked about that word enough. I'm tired of defending myself against accusations from people who don't even know me. I swear, every time I put out a new record, some people just look for reasons to hate me. I guess I usually give them plenty.

Me, Swift, and Bizarre did "Words Are Weapons" for the "Devil's Night" bonus CD. I doubt many people have even heard this one, but Bizarre's verse is sick. He starts talking about Bill Clinton and O.J. and shit. My part was about the gun charges from 2000. That's probably why I sound even more pissed off than usual. It was a fight song. "Shady, stay creative, hold your head up." I was trying to tell myself to keep on writing and stand up for myself. The cops had confiscated my pistol, but I could use my rhymes as bullets.

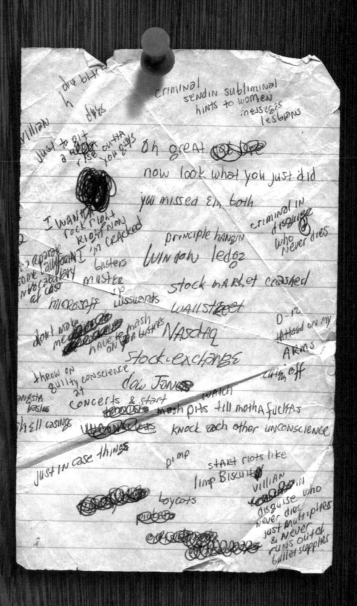

"Stock market crashed. Wall Street. NASDAQ." I have no fucking clue what I was trying to get at. I don't know anything about the stock market, but I see the words "window ledge," so I was probably thinking about people killing themselves because the stock market crashed.

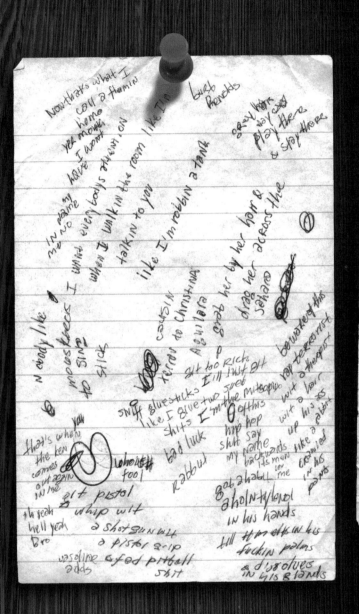

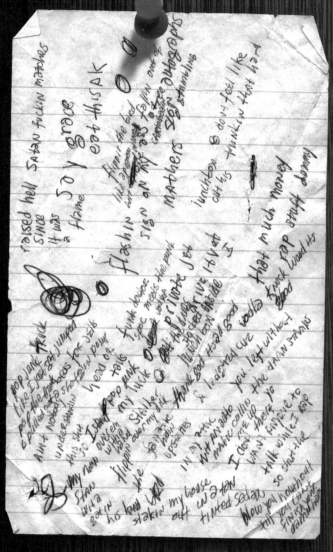

I don't think that enough people heard "Off the Wall," the song I did with Redman. It was a good going-back-and-forth-type thing. "Causin' terror to Christina Aguilera / Grab her by the hair and drag her across the Sahara." I know I used that. That's ill. That's some caveman shit.

I used "My man Stan with a gat in his hand / Stakin' my house out in a damn tinted sedan" in the Redman song too. I was doing so much shit at the time, jumping on every mix tape I could, constantly writing punch lines. It was very draining. I remember being passed the fuck out, searching for shit to say. My dreams are crazy, though, so there's a world of material, even when I'm in snore mode.

It's like a jungle sometimes it makes me wonder why I keep on duckin' under the bed when I hear thunder

cuz I ain't crazy I say shit that's crazy to crazy people to make em believe I'm crazy so they can relate to me & maybe believe in shady so they can be evil baby I like that I'm only as crazy as people made me believe me there'd be just as many motha fuckin' murderers & heroin users without music

I never used these lyrics for anything. I was paying homage to old-school hip-hop. "The Message" was one of the first songs I heard when I was getting into rap. Where it says, "I like that / I'm only as crazy as people made me," I think I meant to say, "*I'm* like that," but I always write in a hurry.

& last week I saw this ... disturb you ... these 3 lil little kids up in the ... movie where ... where he's shooting ... he's shootin all these ... sort of ... so who's ... gotta git ... from row ... bringin the ... not gonna ... screamin ... guns in the ... die ... like violence ... country I couldn't ... together ... smuggle a plastic ... saw him in ... pellit guns ... the hallway ... put your old ... git me off of this ... uncle just look ... off ... operating table ... customs furniture out ... I'm ... guidance aint able ... got no rap & told me ... walk if you just let over ... tape + taught em to swear ... when I me get up ... what about the movie ... asked h ... just lay down okay sir ... bobby ... growin up ... I turned ... nurse whats so tell me ... up worse ... out fine ... his stats stable ... your son doesn't know any ... like Remakin ... were gonna have to cut when ... let his live matha the bw ... a classic ... heard a ... slip Tipper hand me the ... screamin ... before ... upper ... scalpel ... at him ... him up ... 4e 3rd ... unzip get licked liiour fuck ... asshole ... grade ... strip her + shirt work involved was the ... too many ... & fuck her jerkinoff first word ... raps to ... give him some more my life's ... Jimmy Bhan ... gonna die anyway ... like kunta ... & mike ... quite givin us ... what your ... I can't tell shot up bitch ... wifes like ... Mom ... have a seizure before I punch ... Let us live ... they dont give a you in ... fuck up ... VIOLENCE ... these ... the face ... shot fuck about us they's make ... me ... couldn't ... solve tupacs ... you ... I AM ... rich ... I swear to murder ... KIM ... when I get out I'ma ... Hell Freezes ... or I'ma make you ... every ... kill you ... wish I was back flippin ... them god damn hamburgers

0 git me off of this operating table ... I'm stable Jimmy ... the ladder I ... NURSE ... climb on the chimney & try to make some ... look at this cut his ... cuz I'm gt some noise ... KID Hey ... I'm high ... more in my ... break ... Sidney we didnt ... my brain is ... fucked up ... kidneys ... bathroom ... my name is ... in ... did we ... t forgot ... NOPE just ... I'll probably ... let him sit there ... die from ... & shiver & flipped OVER ... in five ... try to deliver ... the sofae ... minutes ... maybe ... collapse & Hot broke both of ... I cant ... last one ... my ass bones ... believe ... collapse ... left shot up in me ... forgot to ... brains ... Breath ... dick ass ... I'm goin to a place ... plumbing kit or ... pretty place ... in his fadin in & funs over the NUNS sober ... ass ... & he's out wobblin the police just runned ... on this back & forth ... OVER the priest ... operatin cuz I'm so ... table layed fucked up off ... IN a range rover ... on his back what I'm on ... the more ... no wonder ... you take it literally ... he can't & I cant ... the more I'ma ... than there aint a man ... say it deliberately ... he cant drink under the ... why this mans stinks ... table no wonder

Near the bottom of the page it says, "Jesus, these motherfuck-ers shot me." I was probably writing a story about being shot. I don't know if the lines connect.

I mention an operating table, like in "Without Me," but there's no connection. These rhymes are crazy old. I can tell by the thoughts behind them, as well as the handwriting. Later on, I started to write smaller and sideways.

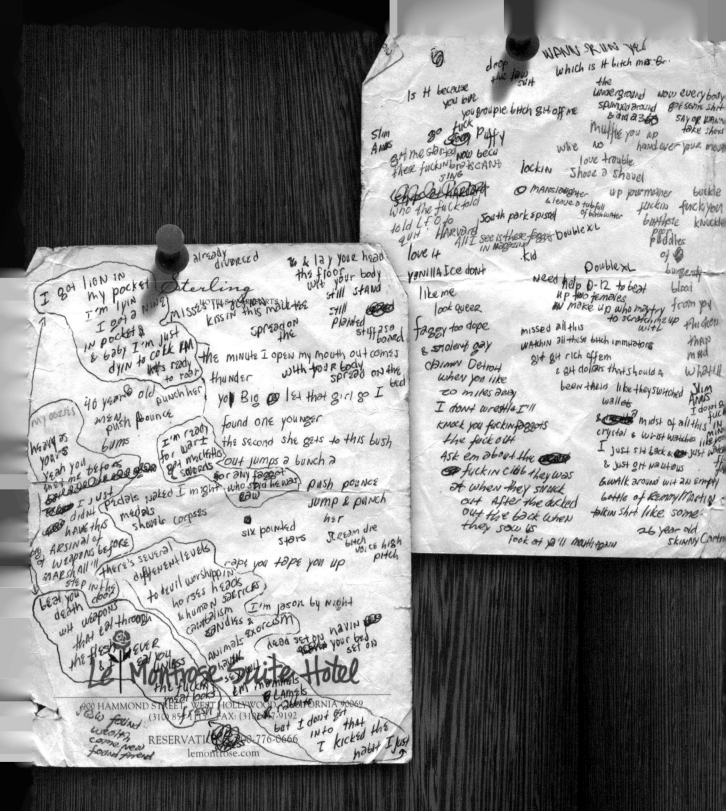

I rapped on a remix of the Notorious B.I.G. song "Dead Wrong."
I remember writing this, literally, in 10 minutes. What Biggie
was saying was so up my alley, and the beat was just so

These are lyrics, scrambled as they may be, from "Marshall
Mathers." At the top, it says, "Drop the lawsuit." Lawsuits
were always on my mind. After your own mother sues you,

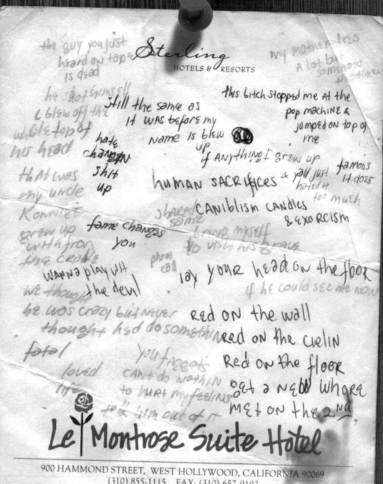

I wrote about Uncle Ronnie's suicide here. He had made a tape of us rapping when we were young, and I wanted to use it on my second album. My family went crazy and wouldn't allow me. They said they were going to sign off, then they weren't, then they were. They made such a big deal out of it. I was just like, "Fuck it." There are also pieces of my verse from Biggie's "Dead Wrong" on here.

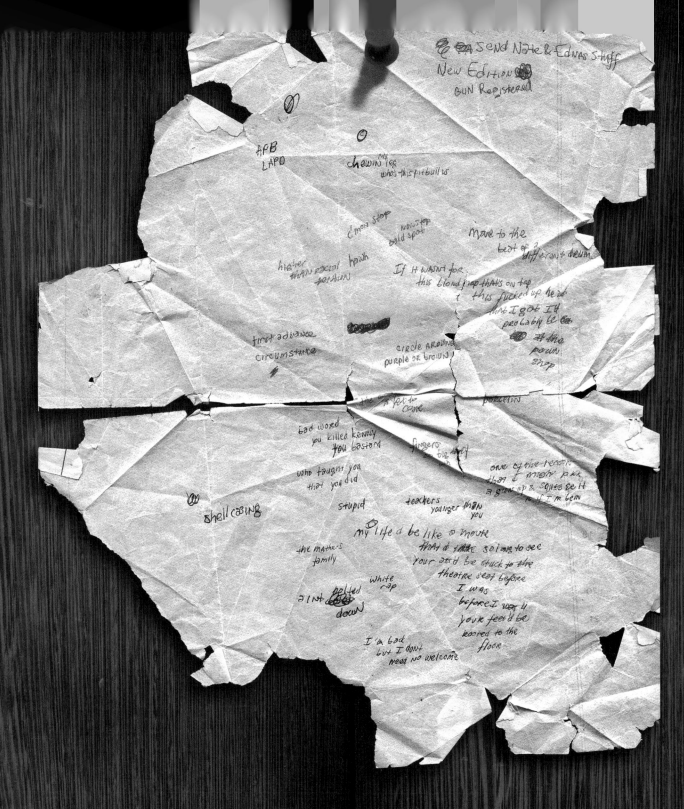

Record Plant is a big recording studio I've worked at out in Hollywood. This page has a lyric from "Drug Ballad" up at the top, and other lines come from a song called "Amityville" on *The Marshall Mathers LP*. When I take lyric sheets into the booth, I go all over the page. Back then, we were using two-inch reels. We didn't have the technological luxury of computerized Pro-Tools. You had to get more down in one take, because if you didn't, you were fucked.

This torn-up paper has notes to myself in the top right corner. "Send Nate Edna's stuff" was about mailing my little brother a birthday card, something from my Aunt Edna. "New Edition" was reminding me to get their CD. "Gun registered"—that meant to get my gun registered. I tried to rhyme "shell casing" on other pages too, once with "gangster basics."

I ndo smoke I never been so broke I'm tossin money right out!
my window today the TV tomorrow the Nintendo goes

sometimes I just don't know why I spend so much dough on
this weed honestly maracajuana seems to be all I wanna see

look at yourself within
A bunch of fuckin punks
I'll fuck every one of you
cockroaches
fuckin pussies
& that slut over there hey bitch
c'mere I wanna fuck
Hi! my name is
I'm famous now come
git some of this dick
platinum
disciple platinum
at some shit
this platinum
c'mon little angry man its time to go home

12 but Marshall you promised me that you'd stop smokin & go git
a job go git a job—you go get a job youre the one who smokes most of
the pot

13 now shut up & roll some pot I need to smoke some pot
you pay the bills — no forgot now shut up & roll some pot

Scott's comin over cunt

hey pauly I know

course earing
Lauren
everybody's
perform Rollin Stone wouldn't like me when girlfriends around me
Source MTV I'm angry star nervous
BET the rebels I'm wearin cycho I stand up in a
Box turn to nike eyes bulge chair & start to give
Hello might look bleached when I'm dry throat a right hook speech
been married for right hook speech cranky then my right could
16 years & he wonder how my/skin turns my hair turns blond earings knock you all out
still uses underground my shirt comes off I a pair of with one swing
a rubber when he fucks you or I want it now sacrifices throw on
& you your boyfriend bodyguard back with los dicks a shots of course I'll never get
tells me everything you of bicardi a Hip Hop quotable in the
slut thats to her thing source
my best friend you make me wanna break past up the girl of course I got shit
had 6 abortions pick up a guitar too on: that I came on at the awards
in 6 months wit I start to
& they weren't like hey this fuckin spill drinks on
his kids 10 guy you're with you, politics
even his kids think he likes you I get this evil little grin
none of my we had 6 hoes on the middle of my
business I think in our teddroom last night chin then I begin cursin
it is 5 o'em that looked just at each & every livin person
were mine you'll 11 like you then all my boys around me start
fuckin bitch you fuckin slut sweatin & gettin nervous
you think your dumb we I stand bussin they balls
husbands faithful right in front of they girlfriends
you should be grateful he
8 aint gave you aids yet he
hates you he dont even
like to touch you

A few of these rhymes come from a song called "Angry Blonde," which I never released. The song was a joke between me and Proof. We were on the Warped Tour, which was basically our first real tour, and we were drinking and experimenting with Ecstasy. Every night, if I didn't actually fight somebody, I would get on the bus and give my "right hook" speech. I'd stand up on the table and go, "My right hook? Oh, I could knock a mother-fucker out. One punch." The next day everybody'd make fun of me, because it was the same speech over and over and over. I used to hit people for the dumbest reasons in the world. I constantly thought that people were saying the wrong thing to me, when half of the time they weren't. My brains were scrambled over-easy for a bit—I can admit it. I'm extremely lucky I didn't get sued more than I did.

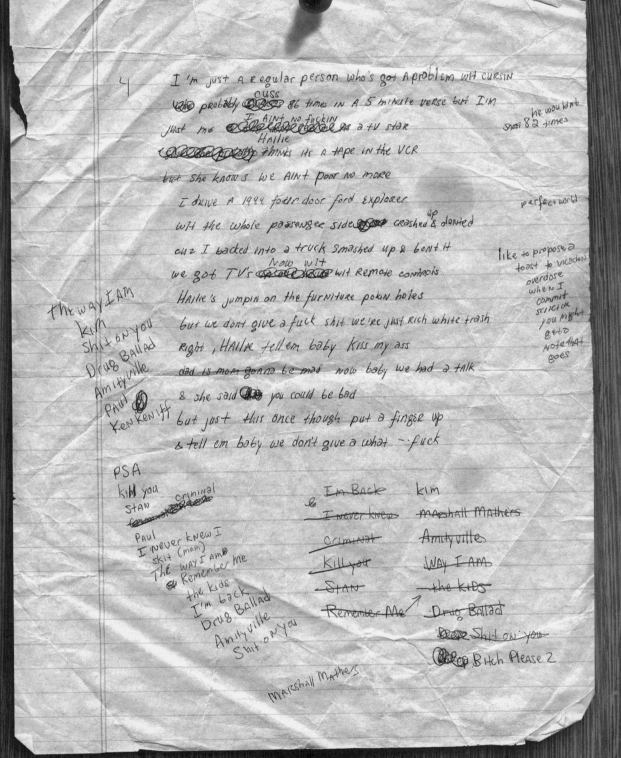

4   I'm just a regular person who's got a problem wit cursin
who probably ~~cuss~~ cuss 86 times in a 5 minute verse but I'm
just me ~~I Aint no fuckin~~ as a tv star   he wouldnt
                    Hailie   shoot 82 times
~~thinks~~ thinks its a tape in the VCR

but she knows we aint poor no more

I drive a 1999 four door ford explorer   perfect world
wit the whole passenger side ~~crashed~~ up crashed & dented
cuz I backed into a truck smashed up & bent it   like to propose a
we got TV's ~~Now wit~~ wit remote controls   toast to vicodin
                                                     overdose
Hailie's jumpin on the furniture pokin holes   when I
                                                     commit
but we dont give a fuck shit we're just rich white trash suicide
                                                     you might
right, Hailie tell em baby kiss my ass   get a
                                                     note that
dad is mom gonna be mad now baby we had a talk   goes

& she said ~~~~ you could be bad

but just this once though put a finger up

& tell em baby we don't give a what ~ fuck

The Way I AM
Kim
Shit on you
Drug Ballad
Amityville
Paul
Ken Keniff

PSA
kill you
STAN   criminal

Paul
I never knew I
            skit (mom)
The Way I AM
    Remember me
    the kids
    I'm back
    Drug Ballad
    Amityville
        Shit on you

                    Im Back   kim
                    ~~I never knew~~ ~~Marshall Mathers~~
                    ~~Criminal~~   Amityville
                    ~~Kill you~~   Way I AM
                    ~~STAN~~   ~~the kids~~
                    ~~Remember Me~~   ~~Drug Ballad~~
                                     ~~Shit on you~~
                                     Bitch Please 2

            Marshall Mathers

Shooting *8 Mile* took me back to the old days, before I had an ego, before I was Eminem, before I was shit. There's a line in the song "8 Mile" about getting stage fright and freezing up. That's something I remember would devastate me. At The Hip Hop Shop, battling was everything. The stage was like a boxing ring. If you won, you were the heavyweight champion. When you were up there, emcees would use personal shit to get at you. If you lived in a trailer park with your mom, or you wore Salvation Army clothes, you'd hear about it. Your life was a gun pointed right at your head. "8 Mile" is my character trying to be a man and find a way out of his situation.

ABCDEFGHIJKLMNOPQR
STUVWXYZ

ABCDEFGHIJKLMNOPQR
STUVWXYZ

I never been in love so much
wit someone or a man or a mates

who must I show
2 bust my flow
2 where must I go
where must I know another

I'm
mylos nerice
sharps dict chunky thick
fish ayry
mattermom
paid
afraid

cross overate
a new bumbo
Rollin over the
bumbo

I just blow
don't I heed 2
my top
somethings get so hot
search
like a butt cuttus
of new enxall me & its

overstep
my boundaries
live in 2 you wouldn't get it
you gone is you the big dall is

this time be come
time
this looks she
sees she moves
paced she breaks
the forgets
made up
mind fuck smile sunday

don't do
well sit I
shit I
don't give dont I gone
@ I know right
where I'm
@ once I'm
over there
down-to-car
I'll never
look back
ain't gon follow

To get the train sound at the beginning of "8 Mile," I sent one of my guys to the railroad tracks that cross 8 Mile Road with a mini recorder and mic. I wanted him to record at the exact location where I used to cross the tracks on my way to school. When I listened to the train effect, we put it on the drum pads, and it almost created the song's melody.

I made "Square Dance" on the set of *8 Mile*. I was working on music between scenes, and I got the idea for the bass line. It kind of sounds like a rock guitar, doesn't it? I mean, in my head it did. I remember running to the studio trailer and humming it to Jeff Bass and Luis Resto. Those guys can pretty much play anything. It always amazed me that I could hum it one time, and they'd get it right away.

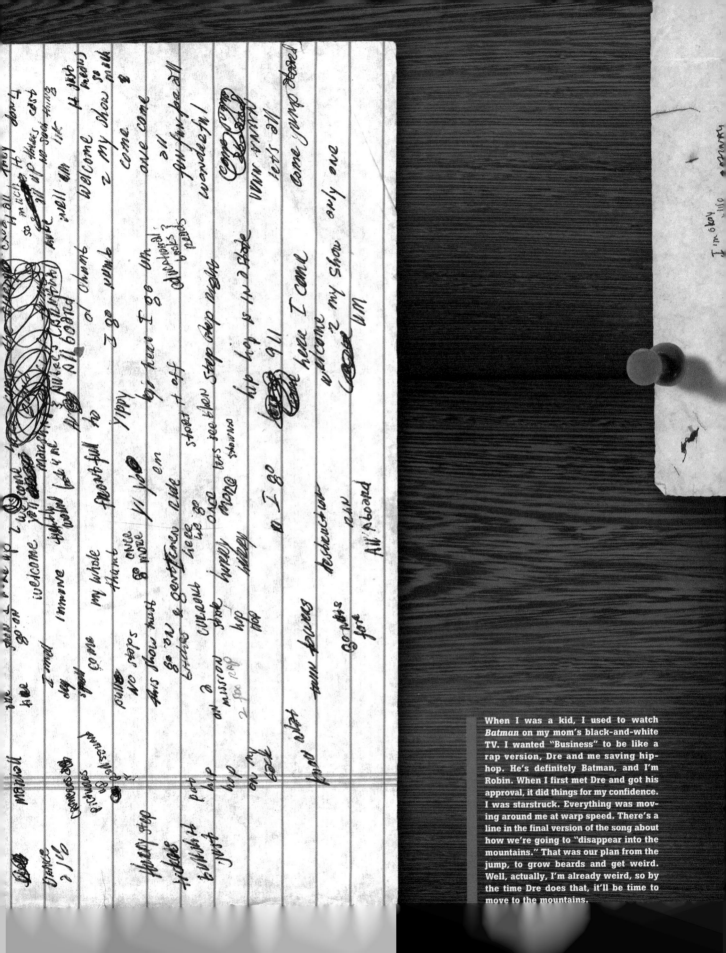

When I was a kid, I used to watch *Batman* on my mom's black-and-white TV. I wanted "Business" to be like a rap version, Dre and me saving hip-hop. He's definitely Batman, and I'm Robin. When I first met Dre and got his approval, it did things for my confidence. I was starstruck. Everything was moving around me at warp speed. There's a line in the final version of the song about how we're going to "disappear into the mountains." That was our plan from the jump, to grow beards and get weird. Well, actually, I'm already weird, so by the time Dre does that, it'll be time to move to the mountains.

Guess who's
back back
again

1
2 sweaters
60 bucks
parmesanmelle

2 pares
ghosts

I'm okay
with my life
so how bout
yours

go back to
@libeers
hey so come
along with me
4 U Z smell what's
cookin

you mime me

plan to see
Terman Dupree

see

if your really
wanna know
what's wrong
wit me

hey there's a concept
that works
20 million or other
white topper
emerge

Millions o peeps
or prints & noodles
since the 90s till

4k is a public
service announcement
traveling & you ∞ in
part by

I
Call on me
I'll be in

nodice it
6k shirt

remember
it's over let go

vintage no bitch don't
throw the switch

paddles
god

sometimes
shell toes
going
down
tha

MTV

bus must mean

well if you

a horse bit a weed mixed wit some
head liquor

move
Chris? MV?
is why me

FCC
want
lot
at
me so
be in

some vodka that II jumpotmer ny
heart yucka than the shook

what?

taket a tablet
you decide pe
know you're
too old let go

off
over
no body
little to chara

like a ...

everybody
anyhow me
need a waste
even controversy
coz it feels
unity

you were to look ot it's
got if you were to look

6th shock out the
hospital

by the doctor
when I'm not
cooperatin

I maybe be shown
know me as shown
just pull III III

media hype
like a ...

keytothe

come on stop

bum
on the
top

when I'm
rockin
the table
while he's

if you could
just ooe path
the gloves &

who's got the
permission

buttyt

fuck cue ou

your

somethimes
itso just remains
light jest gaffe speed
everybody speed the fuckout

operodinate

you wanted stop the
long now stop

whup my refilte

is doot z
& 84 ready

controversy
not the 1st
is sedone

not
beause

heat
what's
already

debating
coz I'm back
it been a little while I am health

kids
go

"Nobody wants to see Marshall no more. They want Shady. I'm chopped liver." I regret saying that in "Without Me," because I'm not chopped liver. When you get famous, fans expect you to act a certain way. I felt like I had to be Shady all the time. It wasn't frustrating—I like being Shady. But I still wanted to talk about the issue in the song. When I made fun of Chris Kirkpatrick and Lynne Cheney, it wasn't genuine anger, I don't think. It was entertainment. Even though *The Eminem Show* was my third album, I still felt like an underground emcee. I struggled with that: what can I say to keep my integrity as a respected emcee? Because I could say anything back in the day at The Hip Hop Shop. Nobody cared. Then you become somebody and all ears are on you.

With "Superman," all I ever hear people talk about is Mariah Carey. Did she inspire it? Yes, she kind of did. I don't want to get into tabloid gossip, but if you read between the lines, and you listen to it, you'll know what I'm talking about. I recorded it toward the end of *The Eminem Show*. I wanted to do it with an LL Cool J kind of a whisper, like in his song "I Need Love." That was the thing for a while with the good old-school love songs, to be gentle and playful with your voice. In "Superman," the girl thinks I'm serenading her, but I'm really telling her I'm sick of her. I'd just gotten divorced from Kim, and I wasn't going down the same road I'd already been on. This was my way of saying, I'm not going to make a love song.

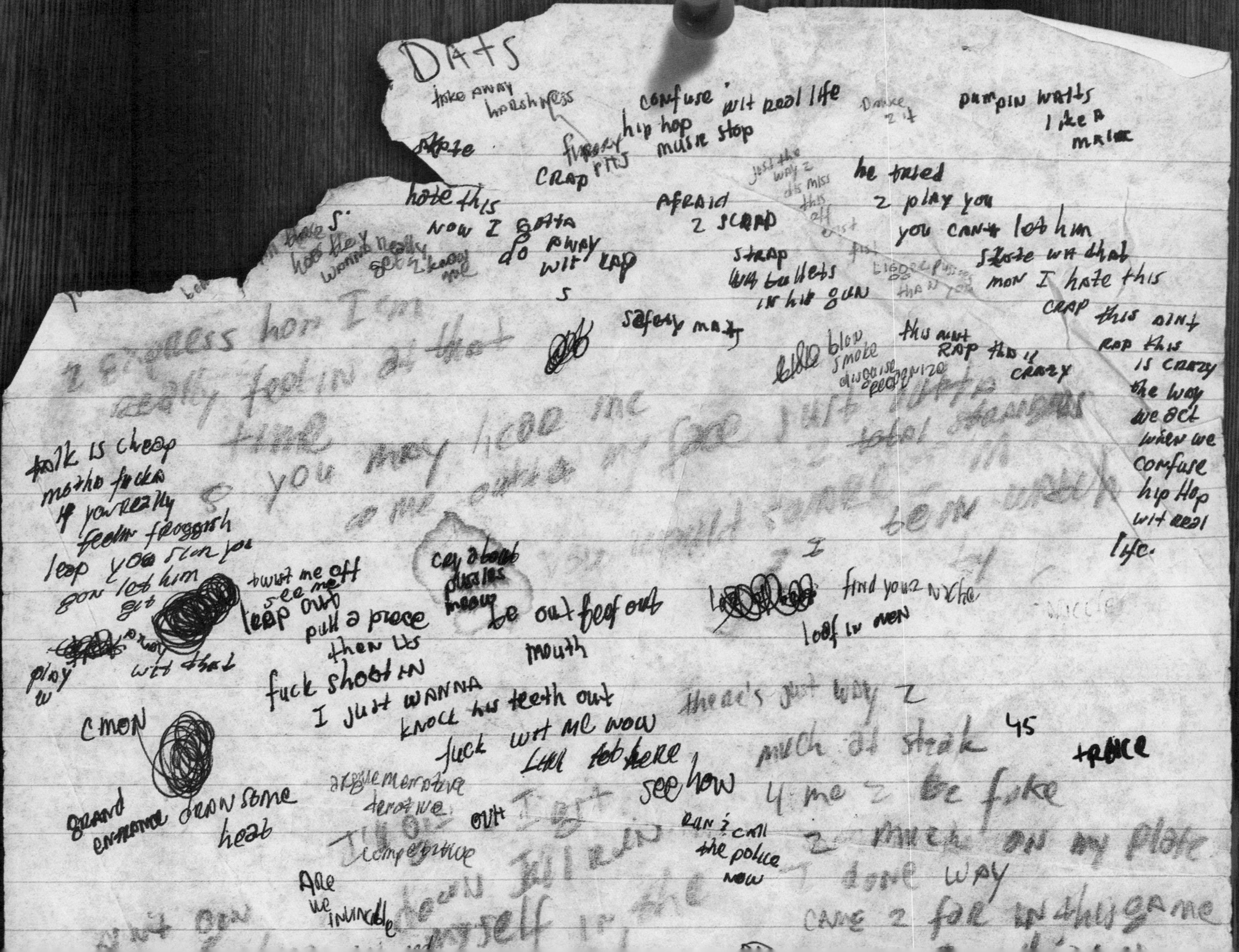

DIATS

take away hopelessness confuse wit real life pimpin hoes
finger hip hop music stop like a man dance it
Akze crap it

hate this he tried 2 play you
now 2 gotta afraid 2 scand you can't lov him
well hey nelly do wit rap strap wit that state wit that
you wanna experience 444 to lets mow I hate this
is his gun crap this aint

safety mat rap this is crazy
kill blon smoke the way
rap this ill we act
when we
confuse
hip hop
wit real
life.

talk is cheep you
marrio fa da I can me
if yourself
feelin fragash
gon lov him trust me off
lep you da sim jus seem
play wit that then its cry down
fuck shon dualls
I just wanna rong 2 out feed out
knoll wit me now
fuck mouth find you wife
c'mon see how street's git way 2 naw is fool
beard oww some a lill tobkere much of steak 45
grandma hoad derotive out see how 4 me 2 be fake +Dtce
the police runican tanca on my plote
Are now done way
we inunde for winthegame

"When the Music Stops" was with D12, and it was definitely a good time for us. We knew we'd made it. To me, the guys had gotten to a new level of rhyming, even better than before. It's one of my favorite rhymes from Proof on a song, and it's one of the best D12 songs. When I was doing my verse, I dropped the beat out for a long time. While I was rhyming, before the beat came in, everybody in the studio had their hands up in the air, going wild. When you get that approval you want to keep going. It was a big-ass party. When Dre came in and listened to it, he was like, "Damn!"

othll

but this bein the new friend
we dont fit in
crackers was out wit
~~African~~ cactus albums blackness was in
African symbols & meditshuns appricers
me & my man Howard & Butter
~~black power~~ & we aint know who's
would go to the mall wit em all over our necks like
we showin em off
not known you
yall even this year'll
that you aint sposed 2 rock
~~home let me grab that and shoot~~ flavor clock
home let me grab that and shoot flavor clock
All I remember's meetin
we gon have 2 should that
back it

Marix's Bassmin sayin how we wrote this
how rough but dope the x clavis tape is
which reminds me back in 89 me
& Kim broke u the 1st time she
was tryin 2 trot time me
& there was this black girl at our
school who thought I was cool cuz I
Rapped so she was kinda eyein me

Me & solo
leans
back
follow

Alright
Byron!
let's go!
the bullshit
enough
let's got it stashed
let's shout doreein this
issue & spew it up
lets take the shit back 2 the
bassmin so we can
discuss statements
that's made our hits
& the whole origin of
the music

Once you reach a certain level, you're a target. People will shit on you. Like when they started flapping their lips about a very old tape from when I was a kid saying the *N* word. I made a song in some kid's basement years ago about a black girl I was dating, after she broke my heart. That song was never intended to be heard by anyone. It was a bad joke that someone tried to use against me years after the fact. Even though I'd already addressed it and apologized, I still wrote the line in "Yellow Brick Road": "I was wrong, 'cause no matter what color a girl is, she's still a ho." I would have to be the most ass-backwards racist ever to mean that word in the way that those losers tried to say I was using it.

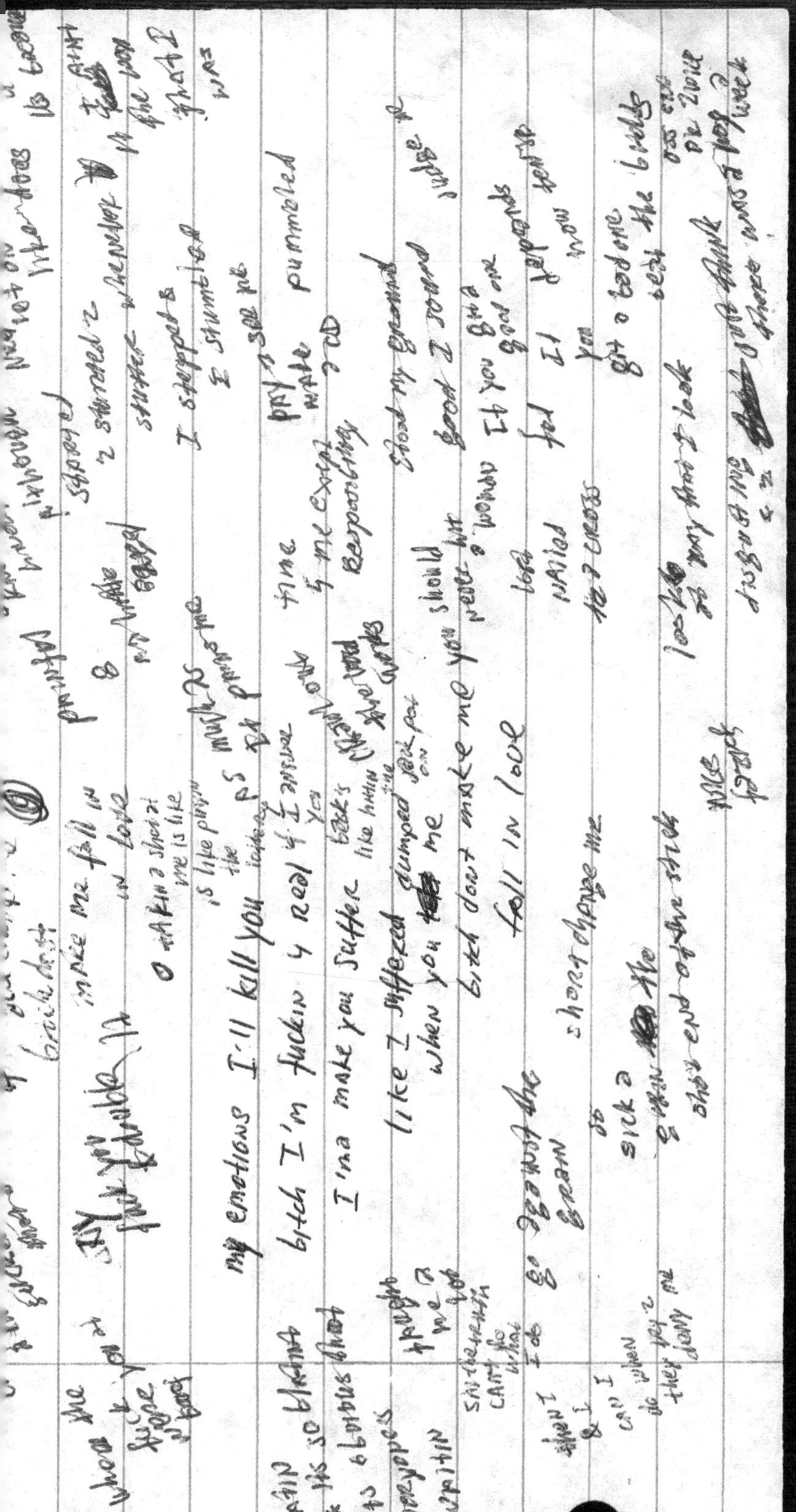

We did "Hey Lady" for Obie's first album, *Cheers.* It might come off like I'm bashing women, but I'm not. It's about the types of girls that would fuck you just to get famous. It's kind of a warning: you may think you know me, because you've bought my records and seen me on MTV, but you don't. If you mess with my emotions, you might wind up stuck with me, and you don't want that.

8

ALL I KNOW, PART 2

IN REAL LIFE, RAP IS ALL
THAT I REALLY KNOW HOW TO DO WELL.

I have a fascination with the movie *Rain Man*, hence my song "Rain Man." That song title came to me in the booth—it wasn't even written on paper. I just said, "Rain Man." What I meant was, this is all I know how to do: rap. I can get in my car and drive, but I don't know how to get places. I don't know north, south, east, west. I'm pretty clueless overall about directions. The song goes, "I don't know how else to put it, this is the only thing that I'm good at." And it's true. I'm always losing my keys, my driver's license. When I went to New York City for gigs, I would get off the subway and end up 14 blocks the wrong way.

When I started working on *Encore*, I was feeling whipped. A pile of my unreleased songs had been leaked—"Bully," "Love You More," "We as Americans." Those songs ended up on the Internet, so I had to start over. We chose to record in Orlando because it was

Wake-up Show," but he didn't even think about producing me before Jimmy Iovine had him listen to my cassette of *The Slim Shady EP*. When me and Dre finally got down to business, we made "My Name Is" and two other tracks on the first day in the studio, and the hooks were instant.

WITH DRE, I WAS LIKE A SPONGE, LEARNING THE TRICKS OF THE TRADE.

I don't think I slept much the first three weeks making *The Slim Shady LP*, all I did was write. I stayed up the whole night writing the verses to "My Name Is," and then came in the next day and recorded. When I nailed a take, Dre'd lean back in his chair and throw his hands up. He'd start clapping and I thought, Holy shit! This is Dre reacting like this to my shit.

The first time Dre ever gave me a full production credit was for "The Way I Am." I was so happy. "The Way I Am" was my rebellion against Interscope asking me to write another pop song. I originally thought "Who Knew" was going to be the first single on *The Marshall Mathers LP*. Dre and I thought the album was done. Then the label wanted to fly me back out to try some more tracks. On the

summer, and it would be a good place for the kids—Dre's and mine. I went down there with nothing, not even a concept. I had the line "You find me offensive / I find you offensive" in my head, and I had no idea where it was going to go from there.

In Orlando, we worked at Lou Pearlman's studio—which was funny because he used to manage all those boy bands like Backstreet Boys and 'N Sync. Dre and I ended up writing 16 songs, and we kept 11 of them. Every time Dre made a beat, I would grab it and go into the next room with it to write. I don't know what it was down there in Orlando—there must have been something in the water. Sometimes Dre and I have these dry spots where he'll come to Detroit to work with me, or I'll go out to L.A. to work with him, and the magic just doesn't happen. But in Orlando, once we got going we just started to fucking fly.

Recording *Encore* reminded me of my very first studio sessions with Dre back in 1998. It's true that Dre might have heard me freestyle on Sway and Tech's show, "The

plane, I got this piano loop in my head, and I wanted to rap right along with it. So that's how I ended up rhyming in that style. I tried a regular beat, and the rhyme just would not go with it, it didn't make sense.

Then Dre explained to me that a lot of the stuff I was doing was actually *producing*. I would go to the Bass Brothers and I would hum stuff to them, but I couldn't

There are a couple of engineers that I work with and some studio musicians. I can't necessarily play the bass, but I can hum out what I'm hearing—the musicians bring it all to life. I can handle the keyboards, though, and my sampler game is mad tight. I really know my way around the studio now.

I didn't know I could scream in a rap song. Dre coached me into expanding. It was like, Dude, you got to capture that emotion.

play it. What Dre taught me was that even when you're just humming a bass line, you're writing music.

Working with Dre really helped me to understand the broad range of the studio—how powerful it is once you grasp the gadgets and doodads. When you know what it is you want, the tools are just an extension of your brain. In the studio with Dre, I was like a sponge, learning the tricks of the trade. I wanted anything I could get out of him, like, "Dre, can I have that old drum kit you don't use anymore?"

When you're in Dre's studio, you get this overwhelming sense of history—the history he's made—and it inspires you to want to make more historic shit. There's so much you have to live up to, working with that man. I still have the feeling I had when I first started working with him. He knows how to maximize my ideas. He sees the creativity in me when I'm not even trying to be creative, and he knows how to get me to put that down on the mic.

Dre also showed me how to do things with my voice

that I had no idea I could do. He had me screaming in the studio! I remember doing the chorus for "Role Model," shouting, "Don't you want to grow up to be just like me?" My throat was hurting. Dre would be, "Again. Do it again." And we stacked a few tracks to make the chorus. If you listen to "Kim," where I'm screaming, you can hear the influence from "Role Model."

I always wanted to make my own beats. I had a vision of getting good enough that by the time I didn't want to rap anymore I could strictly produce. Everyone knows you can't rap forever. Once I got the nod from Dre, I ran with it. Sometimes I prefer working in the studio as a producer. It's inspiring to work with new artists and watch their process. Since I've been where they are, I can help them up when they stumble. I can look into their eyes, see where they're slipping, and fully understand what it takes to get them back on track, whether it's helping to fill in a gap lyrically or changing elements in the mix so words don't get overpowered by sounds. This is hip-hop: the music is there to help accentuate the rhymes.

When I'm working as a producer, like with 50 Cent or Obie Trice or Cashis, I work differently with each artist. The basic routine is to start by making a beat. But there's this struggle as an artist, because there's been music I produced that I've loved so much I really wanted to keep it for myself. Everything I give an artist I'm working with has to be something that I would rap to. I wouldn't

give them anything that I wouldn't want for myself.

I first pitched myself to 50 Cent at a club in Los Angeles. I talked the whole time. There's such a mystique and fear about 50. He told me that sometimes when he goes into corporate meetings he has to smile to make people feel comfortable. 50 is an incredible politician, and when he speaks, he's brilliant. He's one of my favorite lyricists, too. One of my favorite lines of his, from "Hate It or Love It," goes, "Woke up the next morning, niggas done stole my bike." That puts you inside a story. His writing makes you visualize the kind of life this guy had.

50 is a perfectionist. We're similar in that sense. Every single word has to be perfect or I'll trip. But at least you can fix it in the studio. If you fuck up a live show, you're in front of a crowd, and you have to try to laugh it off. Even to this day, if I do a show and I fuck up a word or two in a line, I will sit and dwell on it for that entire night and the next day, until I perform again. Being such a perfectionist, I can't stand to fuck up a couple of words.

Above: I had briefly met 50 once before at the Lyricist Lounge in New York City. I think it was around '98.

Left: In the process of recording Cashis's album, there was a particular beat that I wanted to keep for myself. But Cashis was on such a roll. I thought, I'm going to see what he does with it. And he smashed the beat. He fucking took the beat and ate it. Thank God I didn't keep it for myself.

My first official gig as a producer on my own label was for D12. People perceive D12 as a pop rap group, but that's only because I steered them in that direction on a few singles, like "My Band." If you listen to the lyrics of the first couple of tracks on *D12 World*, you'll see they're not pop at all. Proof used to do mix tapes and say,

"DON'T THINK BECAUSE WE DO POPULAR MUSIC YOU WON'T GET POPPED."

When I first met Swifty, he was in the middle of a fight, just bombing on some dude. We did make some more pop-leaning records here and there—if we had just made gangster records, with the white boy in front, it wouldn't have come off right. So I had to make them adapt to my style. The thing was, I had sold records, and they wanted to sell records. But you'd be surprised. These dudes still have names for

This is me, 50, and Dre at the Shady National Convention. I was nervous as hell. I'd been in the studio so much, and it was my first time getting back out there with the public. The first two, three times, it's nerve-racking, until you fall into a groove where you're used to it again—the lights, cameras, people. When you're recording your record you're in a different mind-set than when you're promoting a record. I'm expected to be funny and on point with everything. I remember kind of not being on point with everything then.

I wonder sometimes if I've reached my pinnacle lyrically, if I'll be able to top what I've already done. Can I get better? But the thing is, the better I get at producing, the more I challenge myself. If I make a beat that's different, I become more interested in seeing if I can come up with something different lyrically.

You know how Jay-Z doesn't write stuff down, he just goes into the booth and spits? Timbaland told me about working with him. Jay would just go into the booth and say, "Okay, let me think for a minute. Okay, punch me here." He would say two lines and then stop. "Okay, give me a minute. Okay, punch me here." I never used to believe that was possible. I found it so hard to believe Jay was spitting with that caliber of rhyme, that there was any way that he could come up with that shit on the spot.

And then I watched our artist Cashis do it. It's a tripped-out method of doing things. You wonder how in the fuck he wrote it that fast.

Sometimes I can slip into that kind of zone where I can write really fast. I've recorded a lot of songs lately where I get a couple of lines in my head and then start freestyling. But my best stuff is when I actually sit down and take the time to write it out. I don't ask myself any questions. Most of my songs start from random thoughts. I get a line in my head and then BOOM. That one line winds up leading to an entire song.

I can rarely sit down with the intention of writing a rhyme and just do it. But when I have an idea, I have to write it on the first piece of paper I can find: I have to get that idea down on paper right then and there, or I'll lose it. Sometimes I look at my old lyric sheets, and I have no idea how I ended up kicking those lines out. I might write an idea down, and it'll end up in a song years later. I try to keep track of rhyme schemes, and I used to copy ones that I liked from one sheet to the next. Then I would take the paper in the booth and kind of go all over the page.

I've been told by other rappers who I greatly respect that I was the first person to put words together that weren't supposed to rhyme—where I flipped the way I was enunciating them. For example, "Look at the store clerk, he's older than George Burns." "Store clerk" and "George Burns" don't rhyme, technically. Or, "I laugh at the sight of death as I fall down a flight of steps and land inside a bed of spider webs." These words don't rhyme, but if you pronounce them right, they do. Some cats in the game have really picked up on that. For instance, "working ball" and "jerking off." It's just an "ur" and "aw," you know what I mean?

Sometimes the ideas don't go anywhere. I was looking at one of my old sheets that simply says "Criminal individual push." I have no idea what that means. I was probably trying to come up with a rhyme and just ended up with a half thought. But I'm particular about what I'll rhyme. I wouldn't rhyme "throat culture" and "black vulture," because "throat" and "black" don't rhyme. You could rhyme "coat vulture" and "throat culture." Or "an occult vulture"? "Cult vulture," "throat culture." I'm just playing with you now.

My writing really suffered after Uncle Ronnie's death, when I was 19. For a whole year I stopped cold. And then, when I did start writing again, the next thing that threw me into a slump was Treach, from Naughty by Nature. He was just so wicked that I considered putting the mic down. I was blown away by his skills. Treach is one of the most slept-on rappers ever. I had this vision of wanting to be the best back then. And if I couldn't be the best, what was the point in rapping?

When I finally stopped worrying and got back into the lab, the first real song I wrote was about Ronnie. It was called "Troublemaker." I rapped as him. I felt he'd been treated like a troublemaker his whole life, so he kind of couldn't help but live up to everyone's expectations.

When I'm in the mind-set, I'll do some writing from my home office. It gets messy sometimes, but there's a method to the madness.

Drawing has always been a way for me to relax. It still is. When I first came out of rehab, it was a good way for me to chill. Doctor's orders: "Do things that aren't super stressful." So I stayed away from the recording studio. I like to draw heroes, I guess. Superheroes, my heroes like Tupac and 50 Cent, and myself, of course.

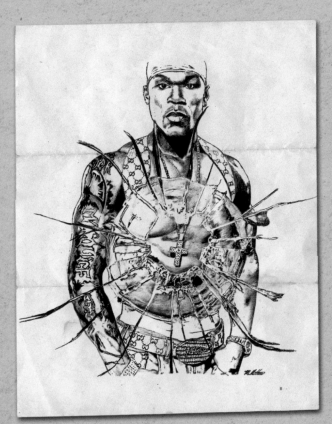

To: Afeni—Your friend 4-ever!
—Marshall

To me, music just doesn't feel like it used to, especially the way it did around the time when 50 Cent first came out. Now, with albums leaking online and the decline of record sales, you just wonder, What the fuck are we doing it for? Nas said hip-hop is dead. I don't think it's dead. It just feels stagnant. Lyrically, it's definitely stagnant. In a lot of the stuff that's out today, the lyrics are simplified.

Music is a job like anything else is. People think that if you make music you're automatically rich, and that ain't true.

The entire industry has changed, and I have no idea where it's going. People are always going to want music—no, they're always going to need music. Which means

THERE WILL ALWAYS BE A PLACE FOR ME IN THIS GAME.

Whether as an emcee, or producer, or, who knows, making movie soundtracks.

Whether I'm someone's favorite rapper or not, whether I'm thought of as one of the best, one of the most half-assed, whatever it is, I am one of the most personal rappers. That's why people relate to me, because people feel like I show so much of myself. That's why random people, like taxi drivers, call me "Marshall." And the reason I put so much of myself out there in the first place is because I had no idea I was going to be so famous. I had no idea, no fucking clue. If I had to do it again, I don't know if I would. I'm glad, though, that my music has brought people together.

I stay at home a lot because I can't go anywhere without a huge entourage. Sometimes I'll go out just to prove that I can do it. I'll leave my neighborhood and go to where a lot of people are—people who have free reign to approach me and ask me for an autograph or take a swing at me, or whatever it is. It's not like I want to stand up in the middle of a restaurant and say, "Hey, look at me!" If you were sitting in a room and the Loch Ness Monster walked in, you might get excited and point and gawk. That's how people react to me—as if I'm not a normal human being. So most of the time I'm cool with staying out of the limelight.

EMINEM
SLIM SHADY EP

ANDY WARHOL
Little Electric Chair
Painting

JIMMY'S BLUES
JAMES BALDWIN

I watch a lot of DVDs, and I watch the same ones so much that it pisses off anyone who's with me. Sometimes I'll watch a Roy Jones DVD, knowing the fucking commentary by heart, and I'll start saying it right along with the guy. Roy Jones, Mike Tyson, Ali—I like to go back and watch that stuff really closely, study it.

I've been recording the new album mainly in the crib. Makes it very easy for me: I just go downstairs. I'm super relaxed. The engineer will be down there hours before me, just getting things right and working out the kinks. It's like the old days, only there's a lot more than a rusty four-track in my basement. I've been having a hard time recording since Proof died. I've got hundreds of songs, though. Stuff that I just make for my own amusement—material just for me and only me.

I try not to have too many people around when I'm working; I don't want anyone to peep in on my process. Being in the studio is sometimes fun, but it isn't necessarily fun. It's work, it's my craft. If you have too many dudes in there smoking blunts and acting silly it becomes hard to think and get straight answers. You wind up with a bunch of high dudes saying, "That shit is dope, Em!" Or girls just wanting to be girls. Which is nice, of course. Just not when I'm working.

RAP FORCED ME TO DEAL WITH PEOPLE SOCIALLY. IT FORCED ME TO GET OFF MY ASS AND SHOUT SHIT AT PEOPLE.

It felt good. Hip-hop was a community where I could fit in, and it really didn't matter that I was white. Hip-hop made me feel like I was on a team. I felt like I was not only representing people who had my back, but also connecting them to each other. That's what hip-hop is all about for me. Always has been.

Nimms / Vickery / Splash News: p. 6 (bottom left, bottom right)

Estevan Oriol: p. 68 (bottom right), p. 122 (second row middle), p. 123 (top right), p. 194, p. 204-205

AP Photo / Carlos Osorio: p. 6 (top right, top left), p. 9, p. 106 (middle right)

© Stuart Parr: p. 69 (second row middle), p. 122 (middle right)

Bill Pugliano / Liaison: p. 129

Louis Quail / Camera Press / Retna Ltd.: p. 35

Eli Reed / Universal Pictures: p. 102, p. 108-109, p. 112-117

Courtesy of *Rolling Stone*: p. 61

Pierre Roussel / Newsmakers: p. 74

© Paul Rosenberg: p. 42, p. 68 (top middle, bottom left), p. 69 (top left, bottom right), p. 122 (second row left)

Patrik Rytikangas : p. 27, p. 29 (top right, bottom right)

Nathan Sayers: p. 64-65

© Michael Schreiber: p. 191 (top right)

Courtesy of Shady Records: p. 19, 20 (left), p. 26, p. 27, p. 29 (top right, bottom right), p. 34, p. 58-59, p. 64-65, p. 67, p. 68 (top right, middle), p. 69 (middle left, third row middle, third row right), p. 103, p. 126, p. 190 (top), p. 138, p. 148

SKAM2?: p. 22-23

Steven Tackeff / ZUMA Press: p. 43 (bottom)

Charley Valley / Sipa Press: p. 135, p. 139

Lyndon Wade: p. 32-33, p. 38-39

Scott Webster / Windsor Star / ZUMA Press: p. 134

WENN: p. 20 (right), p. 21 (right), p. 140 (top left, bottom right, bottom left), p. 149 (top)

Kevin Winter / Getty: p. 89

DUTTON

Published by Penguin Group (USA) Inc.

375 Hudson Street, New York, New York 10014, U.S.A.

Penguin Group (Canada), 90 Eglinton Avenue East, Suite 700, Toronto,
Ontario M4P 2Y3, Canada (a division of Pearson Penguin Canada Inc.);
Penguin Books Ltd, 80 Strand, London WC2R 0RL, England; Penguin
Ireland, 25 St Stephen's Green, Dublin 2, Ireland (a division of Penguin
Books Ltd); Penguin Group (Australia), 250 Camberwell Road, Camberwell,
Victoria 3124, Australia (a division of Pearson Australia Group Pty Ltd);
Penguin Books India Pvt Ltd, 11 Community Centre, Panchsheel Park,
New Delhi - 110 017, India; Penguin Group (NZ), 67 Apollo Drive, Rosedale,
North Shore 0632, New Zealand (a division of Pearson New Zealand Ltd);
Penguin Books (South Africa) (Pty) Ltd, 24 Sturdee Avenue, Rosebank,
Johannesburg 2196, South Africa

Penguin Books Ltd, Registered Offices: 80 Strand, London WC2R 0RL,
England

Published by Dutton, a member of Penguin Group (USA) Inc.

First printing, October 2008

10 9 8 7 6 5 4 3 2 1

Photo, illustration, and other image credits, constituting an extension of
the copyright page, appear on pages 206–207.

REGISTERED TRADEMARK—MARCA REGISTRADA

Library of Congress Catalog Card Number: 2008927717

ISBN 978-0-525-95032-5

Set in Clarendon, Aachen Bold, and City

Printed in China

Produced by

 MELCHER
MEDIA

124 West 13th Street
New York, NY 10011
www.melcher.com

Publisher: Charles Melcher
Associate Publisher: Bonnie Eldon
Editor in Chief: Duncan Bock
Executive Editor: Lia Ronnen
Production Director: Kurt Andrews

Project Editor: Lauren Nathan
Editorial Assistant: Daniel Del Valle

Designed by Paul Kepple and Scotty Reifsnyder
@ Headcase Design
www.headcasedesign.com

Special thanks to Marshall B. Mathers III,
Sacha Jenkins, Paul Rosenberg, and Luca Scalisi.

Thanks also to Bronwyn Barnes, Adam Bright,
David E. Brown, Karin Catt, Daniel Del Valle,
Max Dickstein, Marc Gerald, Coco Joly, Trena
Keating, Lily Kosner, Liana Krissoff, Marc
LaBelle, Maurice Malone, Ian Marshall, Tracy
McNew, Lisa Milton, Stuart Parr, Kenneth
Partridge, Ian Preece, Anna Rabinovitch, Holly
Rothman, Jessi Rymill, Patrik Rytikangas,
Nathan Sayers, Skam, Lindsey Stanberry,
Shoshana Thaler, Alex Tart, Brian Tart,
Vanessa Vellucci, Anna Wahrman, Rebecca
Wiener, Betty Wong, and Megan Worman.

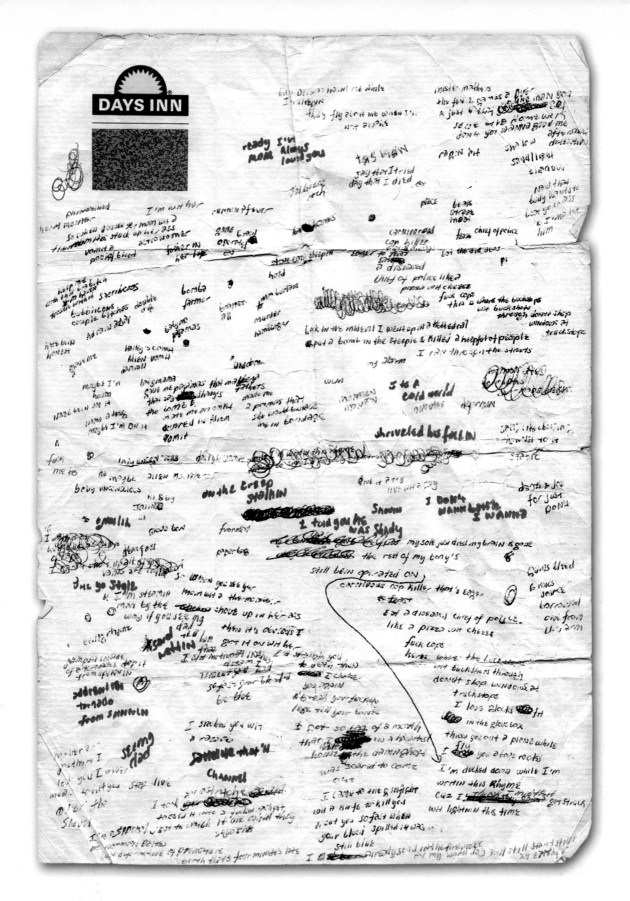

"My Name Is," Burbank, Calif., 1998.

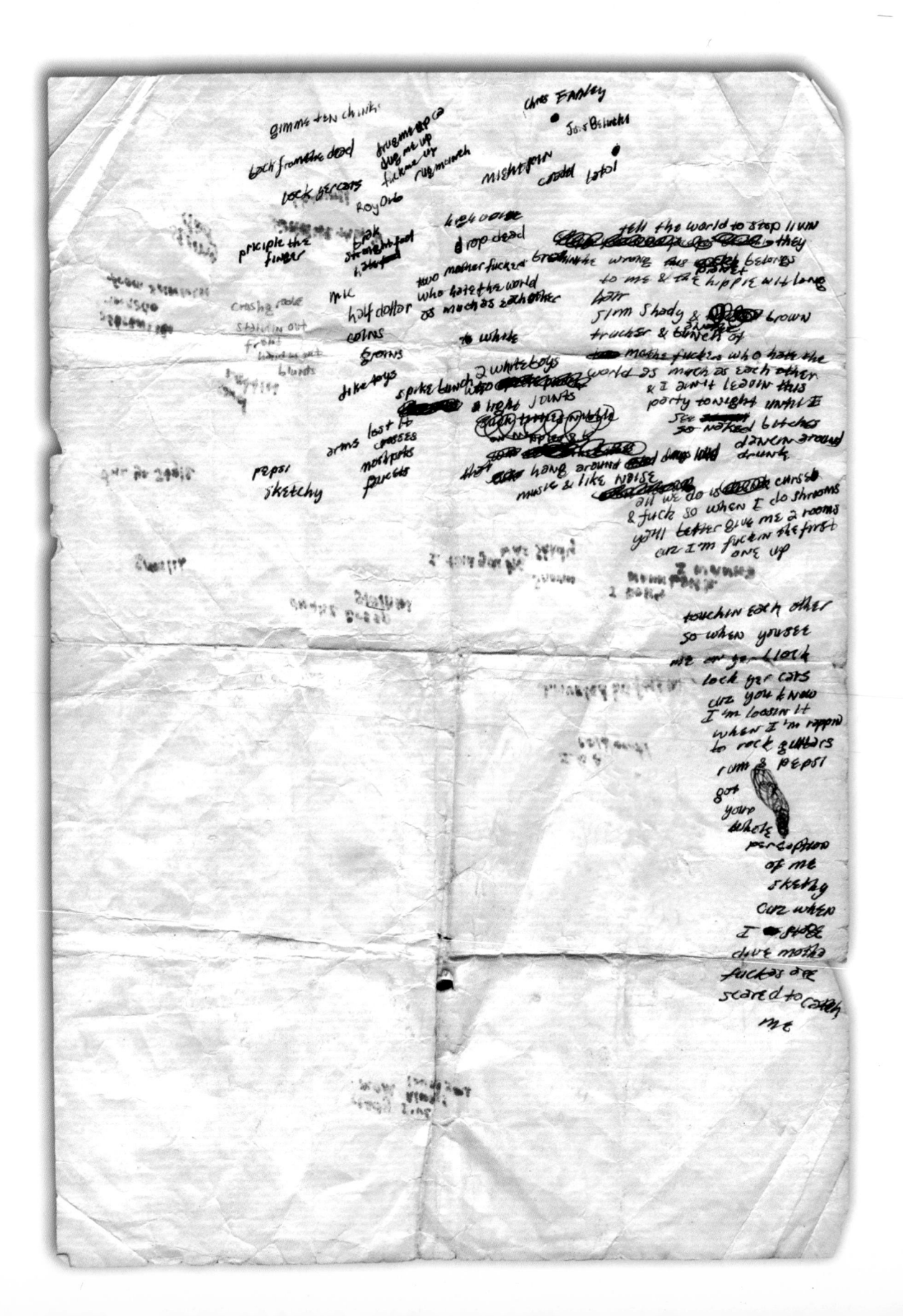

gimme ten chinkis

Chris Farley
● Joe Beluski

lock fromthe dead   drug me up ©
                     dug me up
lock her cats   fuckme up   rugmunch   mishtjoin   coded lotol
              RoyOrb

principle the finger   Djak   hee oouie
                        straightfoot   drop dead   tell the world to stop livin
                        t.shaped   they
                                        two motherfuckers breathine wrong this belongs
                        mic   planet
crashing roole   half dollar   who hate the world   to me & the hippie wit long
startlin out   as much as each other   hair
front   coins   jimm shady & brown
hands out   to white   trucker & bunch of
blunts   grons
dike toys   motherfuckers who hate the
             spike lunch 2 whiteboys   world as much as each other
                                       & I aint leadin this
             arms lost it & head jonas   party tonight until I
pepsi   see so naked betches
sketchy   crosses   dancin around
             hot pockets that can hang around songs loud   drunk
             fucels   music & like noise
                                       all we do is cursse
                                       & fuck so when I do shrooms
                                       yoll better give me a rooms
                                       cuz I'm fuckin the first
                                       one up
                                       I never
                                       I saw

                                       touchin each other
                                       so when youset
                                       me on go block
                                       lock for cats
                                       cuz you know
                                       I'm loosin it
                                       when I'm rappin
                                       to rock guitars
                                       rum & pepsi
                                       got
                                       your
                                       whole
                                       perception
                                       of me
                                       sketzy
                                       cuz when
                                       I state
                                       dive motda
                                       fuckes are
                                       scared to catch
                                       me

this is the last letter I'ma write

Dear Slim
you still aint called back or not
or wrote I aint mad I just think
I hope you have a chance   It fucked up
                                        that you dont answer fans
                                        he was such a good kid

If you don't wanna talk to me outside   things that fast bad to make   back to do   5th of vodka
when I'm gone   your concert you didnt   eggs not the   A show   problem   got problem

I can relate to what you're sayin in your songs so when I have a shitty day   have to probably was a problem   world was on   I'm not   Hallway   saw me   envelop
but you coulda signed an autograph for arnie joshua   with the postage   mental patient   between complete alcoholic   still CALLIN me
I drift away & passin on   prodly lestan anyway

I dont really got shit else so that shit helps when I'm depressed   Who'd ve ever thought we'd do some que together   daughter you'd ve Never thought   DEAR   Slim   but you   I wrote my home phone on the bottom   sent two back in Autumn   you must   got Em
I'd   the   I wrote you back   and my cell my pager
I even got a   I   sloppy on
tatoo of your name across the chest   baked potato fake tomato bacon egg &   MAN I'M SORRY   I had a friend kill   there probably was a problem wit the envelope
sometimes I even cut my wrist   steak & eggrolls cake & bagels   himself OVER some S   did n't want him
you to see how much I'll bleed just like   Liech who   I know you probably
though I just don't like bein lied to   Add zen slim   the pain   I know you probably hear this everyday but   sometimes I
remember when we met in denver   you said if I write such a fan   rush/hear   skribble adresses to sloppy when I
I get so bored & lonely just to chat   you would   write back so I'm just like   I'm you biggest fan
                  you in a way   I never knew   I even got the underground
                  my father   another   shit that you did wit scam
see everything you say is real & I respect you caz   so much grows up   6   to always cheat YOUR posters and your pictures man   CRESENT heights mom & bed dressed in florescent her whites   I like the shit you did w it Rawkus too   that shit was bad   anyways I hope   Got Em
                                    Lot Anyways
                                    fuck it whats been up man
you tell what I thought maybe   how's your daughter
my girlfriend not so bad   my girl friends present too
gets jelous got so mad caz I talk about   I'm bout to be a father
you 24/7   It is a must that I bust Any gun you hand   you git this man   3   If I have a daughter guess
but she dont know sabotaged dad divorced   put the in the gun than   hit me back just to chat   what I'ma caller what I'ma name her
you like I know you No one does   Brandon   SINCERELY yours   I'm a name her
she dont what it was like for people like us growin up   Lee   you gotta call your biggest fan   this is this   you'll ever   RONNIE
that's my brother   girl friends NERVOUS   me man I'll be the   biggest fan   lose sincerely yours   I Read about your uncle RONNIE
man he's only 6 years old waited in the blistein cold   that's pretty shitty man you like his fuckin idol he wants to be just like you man he likes you more than I do   I'm not that mad
for you for 4 hours & you just said no

L2000.23.2

"S t a n,"   L o s   A n g e l e s,   2 0 0 0.

Dear Stan
I meant to write
you ~~sooner~~ but I've just
been busy
you said your girlsfriend
pregnant now how far
along is she

forgot
to call

& In the car they found
a tape but it didnt
say who it was to
come to think about it
his name was —
it was you

look I'm really flattered
you would call your daughter
that & here's an autograph
for your brother I
wrote it on ~~the~~ a
starter cap

SKRIBBLIN
Rain windshield
car crashin gate
goin over BRIDGE
hittin water
Girl screamin
from trunk

fuckin
ISSUES
fuckedup is you

throw
a bitch
off a bridge
locked inside
a fridge

& sorry I aint see
you at the show
I must've missed you
don't ~~think~~ I did the
shit intentionally just
to diss you
but what's the shit you
said about you like to
cut your
& you scream about it   wrist

Dear mister I'm too good to call or write
~~my~~ fans
this'll be the last ~~package~~ I ever SEND
your ass
its been 6 months & still no
~~word~~ I dont deserve it
I know you got ~~my~~ last two letters
I wrote the adresses on em perfect
so this is a cassette I'm sendin
you I hope you hear it
I'm in ~~my~~ car right now
I'm doin 90 on a freeway

hey slim I drank a fifth
of vodka

You know
~~there's~~ the song
by Phil Collins in the
air of the night
about ~~that guy~~ that guy
could've saved the
other guy from
drownin
but didn't & Phil
saw it all then
at a show he
found him
that's kinda
like this is you
could've rescued
me from drownin
Now its too late
I'm on a thousand
downers
& all I wanted
was a lousy letter
or a ~~phone~~ call
I hope you no
I ripped all of
your picturss off
the wall

I say that shit ~~
JUST CLOWNIN

read this
letter

you got some
issues Stan I
think you
need some
counselin
to keep your
ass from
bouncin off the
walls when you
get down
some

I just dont
want you to do
some crazy
shit I seen
this one shit
on the news
a couple weeks ago
that made me sick
some dude was drunk
& drove his car over
a bridge & had his
girlfriend in the
trunk & she was
pregnant with his
kid

I hope your CONSCIENCE eats
at you & you can't ~~sleep~~ without
me
ss

c'mon how fucked
up is you
~~
~~ you got some
ISSUES ~~
~~ slim
shut up bitch I'm tryin to talk
hey slim that's my girlfriend
screamin ~~
~~ in the TRUNK

& what's the other
shit about us meant
to be together
thats type of shit'll makes
me not want to
meet each other

I really think you girlfriend
need each other

maybe you just need to
treat her better I hope
you get to read this
letter I hope it reaches
you in time before you hurt yourself
~~
~~ I
think you'll be ~~doin~~ doin just
fine if you relax a little
I'm glad I inspire you but Stan
why're you so mad try to understand I do want
you as a fan

but I aint slit her throat I
just tied her up ~~
~~ I aint
like you cuz
If she suffocates she'll
suffer more & then she'll
die too
well gotta go I'm almost
at the bridge now
oh I forgot ~~how can I~~
sposed ~~
~~ send this shit
out

I loved you slim
we could've ~~
~~
think about it
you ~~ruined~~ it
Now ~~
~~ I hope
you go to sleep
& dream about
it & when
you dream I hope
you cant sleep

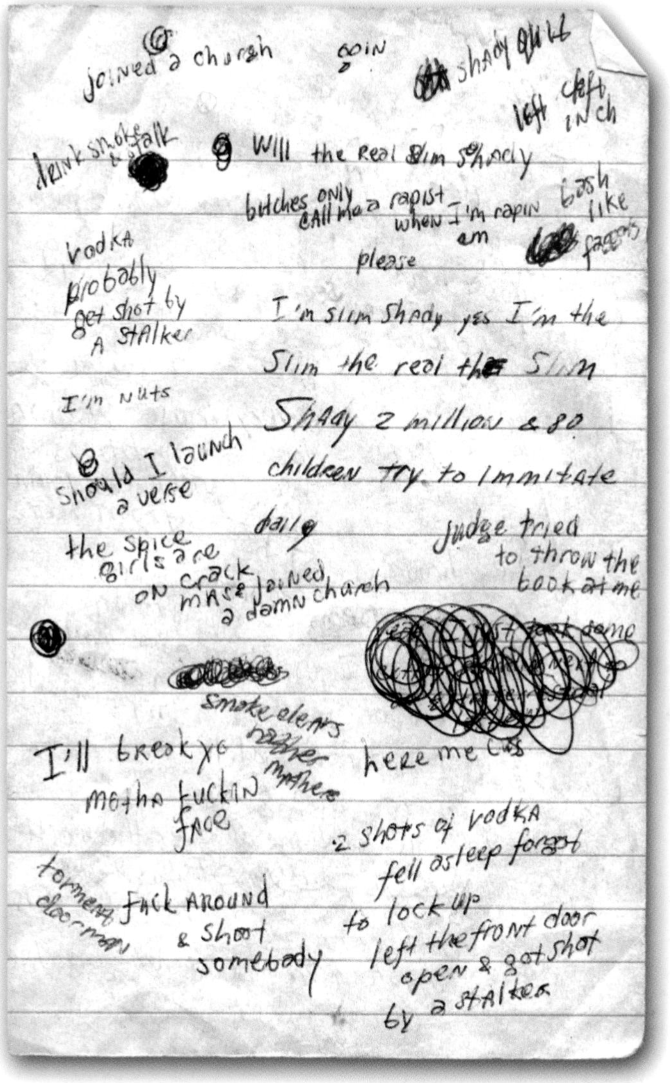

joined a church

goin

shady

left

inch

drink smoke & talk

Will the real Slim Shady

bitches only

call me a rapist

when I'm rapin

bash

like

am

please

vodka

probably

get shot by

A stalker

I'm Slim Shady yes I'm the

Slim the real the Slim

Shady 2 million & 80

children try to immitate

daily

I'm nuts

should I launch

a verse

judge tried

to throw the

book at me

the spice

girls are

on crack

mase joined

a damn church

I'll break yo

motha fuckin

face

here me cus

2 shots of vodka

fell asleep forgot

to lock up

left the front door

open & got shot

by a stalker

fuck around

& shoot

somebody

"The Real Slim Shady," Los Angeles, 2000.

O   every chair   O

I quit
I'm sick   Hi my NAME is dizzy
of this
op shit I   speaRs
don't like it   see my ears I used to
I git to pissed
off over this   be a mousketeeR
mic   Now I got AN album
                every house CAN hear
                look at my titties
                you can see em bounce
                            from here

hey how you   FBI
doin ██████████   came through
                   & left me dry
look At me I just   but guess what
got A boob job   I'm
                   they let me slid

but I'm a role model
for teenage girls
people love me all over the world
████████████████████████
okay Now WAIT you see this
mascara
look I'm PristiNA aguilar

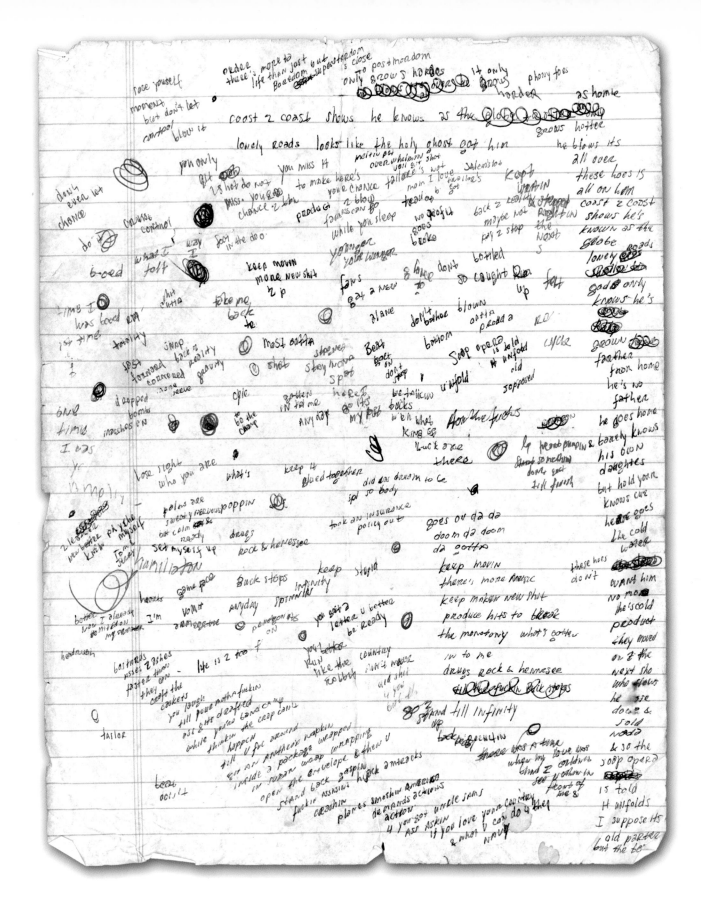

"Lose Yourself," Detroit, 2002.

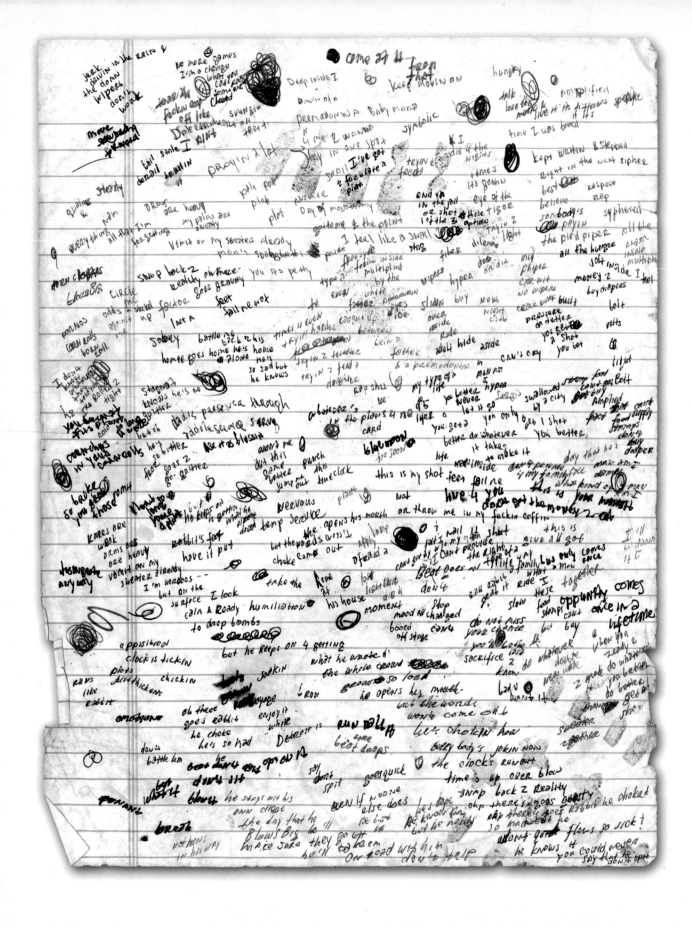

OCT 2 2008

I'M BIGGEST

I EVEN GOT TH SHIT THAT YOU

I OWN MY

YOUR POSTER

PICTURES

SHUT U 2 SNEAK ME IN

in front of the club with the

LOYALTY

UR the ONE the MAN

AMERICAN

RAPE GAME

DEEP PILLS

6 IN